Who Are You Without Colonialism?
Pedagogies of Liberation

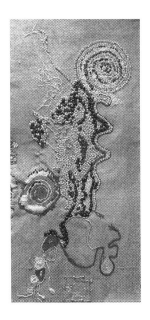

A Volume in:
Curriculum and Pedagogy Series

Series Editor:
The Curriculum and Pedagogy Group

A Volume in:
Curriculum and Pedagogy Series

Series Editor:
The Curriculum and Pedagogy Group

BOOKS IN THE SERIES

BIPOC Alliances: Building Communities and Curricula (2022)
Indira Bailey, Christen Sperry García, Glynnis Reed, & Leslie C. Sotomayor II

The Kaleidoscope of Lived Curricula: Learning Through a Confluence of Crises 13th Annual Curriculum & Pedagogy Group 2021 Edited Collection (2021)
Karin Ann Lewis, Kimberly Banda, Martha Briseno, & Eric J. Weber

Making A Spectacle: Examining Curriculum/Pedagogy as Recovery From Political Trauma (2020)
Megan Ruby, Michelle Angelo-Rocha, Mark Hickey, & Vonzell Agosto

*Ideating Pedagogy in Troubled Times:
Approaches to Identity, Theory, Teaching and Research* (2019)
Shalin Lena Raye, Stephanie Masta, Sarah Taylor Cook, & Jake Burdick

Critical Intersections In Contemporary Curriculum & Pedagogy (2018)
Laura Jewett, Freyca Calderon-Berumen, & Miryam Espinosa-Dulanto

Collective Unravelings of the Hegemonic Web (2014)
Becky L. Noël Smith, Katherine Becker, Libbi R. Miller,
Natasha S. Reid, & Michele D. Sorensen

Liminal Spaces and Call for Praxis(ing) (2013)
Miryam Espinosa-Dulanto, David L. Humpal, Leilya Pitre, & Jolanta Smolen Santana

Excursions and Recursions: Through Power, Privilege, and Praxis (2012)
Brandon Sams, Jennifer Job, & James C. Jupp

*Surveying Borders, Boundaries, and Contested
Spaces in Curriculum and Pedagogy* (2011)
Cole Reilly, Victoria Russell, Laurel K. Chehayl, & Morna M. McDermott

Who Are You Without Colonialism? Pedagogies of Liberation

Clelia O. Rodríguez
Josephine Gabi

INFORMATION AGE PUBLISHING, INC.
Charlotte, NC • www.infoagepub.com

Library of Congress Cataloging-In-Publication Data

The CIP data for this book can be found on the Library of Congress website (loc.gov).

Paperback: 979-8-88730-426-7
Hardcover: 979-8-88730-427-4
E-Book: 979-8-88730-428-1

Copyright © 2023 Information Age Publishing Inc.

All rights reserved. No part of this publication may be reproduced, stored in a retrieval system, or transmitted, in any form or by any means, electronic, mechanical, photocopying, microfilming, recording or otherwise, without written permission from the publisher.

Printed in the United States of America

OFFERINGS

The Fading Echoes of 'Decolonising Education' ix
Josephine Gabi

Cintli viii

Chihera Shava Mhofu: Libation Offering to Ancestors 1
Faith Mkwesha

I Am Who I Am 9
Pamela Lynn Chrisjohn

Dai pasina hupambepfumi ndiri ani? 13
Josephine Gabi

Land/Home Dreaming 19
Glenda Mejía

The Night I Fell Into the Stars 23
Mary Chakasim

Who Are You ~~Without Colonialism?~~ 33
Jihan Thomas

v

vi • CONTENTS

Within the Me 35
Anthony C. Guerra

Time Immemorial 39
Amanda Buffalo

liberation 43
c.k. samuels

A Love Letter to Myself 49
Jackie Lee

Shauna Landsberg 53
Shauna Landsberg

unscripted 67
Künsang

13 Moons o o o o o o o o o o o o o o 77
Danielle Denichaud

Without Colonialism I Am 81
Ram Trikha

The Body is an Altar Unaltered 83
Hope Kitts

Deadlines / Dead-Lines / Đét-Lai. Đét-Lai / ....
Dead-Lines / Deadlines 87
Trung M. Nguyễn

Qué sería yo y este mundo sin la Colonización 93
Odaymar Cuesta

Unrooting the Colonial Seed 99
Karthik Vigneswaran

▮▮▮▮▮▮ Root, ▮▮▮▮▮▮▮▮▮▮▮▮
Shadow-Work as Pedagogical Training 103
Zahra Komeylian

without colonialism 115
Aquib Shaheed Yacoob

Remnants of the In-Between 121
Anthazia Kadir

BlaC Altar 123
Kay Williams

... walking the forgotten path... 131
Miryam Espinosa-Dulanto

A Micro-Essay on the "Micro-Essays on Poetics" 135
Octavio Quintanilla

I'm a Coast Salish Punjabi Settler and I am Not Okay 137
Sonia Das

... : I am you : past : present : future : You are me :
Lak'ech : 143
Clelia O. Rodríguez

Bios/Statements From Contributors 151

CINTLI

Artist: Irvin R. Chrisjohn 1924–1985. Title: Lotiskle: wake' (They—Bear Clan—are looking after the well being of the nation). Private collection. Date carved: 1981. Location: On^yota'a:ka (People of the Standing Stone) Oneida Nation of the Thames. Photographer: Kalihwisaks aka Pamela Chisjohn.

OPENING NOTE

The Fading Echoes of 'Decolonising Education'

Josephine Gabi

Embracing principles of transparency and openness, I reflect on my experience as a co-editor from a haunting task of co-editing a book about 'decolonising education' that did not materialise to 'Who are you without colonialism?,' a book that took me on a path to thinking deeply about who I am without colonialism as a liberatory pedagogy of disentangling myself from the tentacles of coloniality. I am overwhelmed with gratitude as I write this Opening Note. It is an honour that I am standing on the shoulders of an ancestor in the making, Dr. Clelia O. Rodríguez—a protector of our sacred knowledges.

It all started as an invitation by a colleague to act as a co-editor of a book about 'Decolonising Education,' an idea that emanated from an ardent desire to challenge the entrenched colonial residues that still linger in higher education whilst envisioning a future that is free from the logics of colonialism and coloniality. The prospect of instigating transformative change in higher education captivated me. With clarity of thought, together with my co-editors, we carefully crafted a 'traditional' call for papers, casting our net far and wide, across our professional networks. The response reinforced our belief in the book's timeliness and significance in confronting the challenges of 'decolonising education.' The resonance of the topic with fellow academics was unsurprising. 'Decolonising education' has

---

Who Are You Without Colonialism? Pedagogies of Liberation, pages ix–xii.
Copyright © 2023 by Information Age Publishing
www.infoagepub.com
All rights of reproduction in any form reserved.

become a 'hot' topic in academic discourse, and our proposed book encapsulated the urgency and essence of this dialogue.

Despite the initial momentum, we encountered a pivotal juncture when two of our esteemed colleagues, who helped shape the initiative, departed for diverse reasons. Yet, this opened the possibility of finding a new co-editor. Embracing the challenge with determination, my colleague invited Dr. Clelia O. Rodríguez to take on the role of lead editor. To our delight, Dr Clelia O. Rodríguez embraced this responsibility with Humility and Respect. Through rigorous deliberation and discernment, we had meticulously curated a selection of abstract contributions that aligned with our aspirations for 'decolonising education.' We shared our carefully curated book chapter abstracts with Clelia, anticipating she would find them compelling and inspiring hope for a possible anticolonial future. We were conscious of Sabelo Ndlovu-Gatsheni's (2017, p. 32) observation that "decolonisation encapsulates possibilities of creating another world, embedded in it are colonial wounds crying out for healing." We were confident of our rigorous 'selection' process and were keen to meet with Dr. Clelia O. Rodríguez to discuss her thoughts on the abstracts. "Decolonisation is dead!," "Decolonising education is dead!" she says, "and so is the language used in all these abstracts to talk about it. Words such as '*exploration*' and '*discovery*' are tools that carry harmful colonial ideologies that continue to distort, marginalise, inferiorise and erase the histories, knowledges and experiences of indigenous communities." Dr. Rodríguez told us: The 'master's tools will never dismantle the master's house.' (1984, p. 19). Minna Salami (2020, p. 34) echoes it when she says that:

> To determine what tools to discard, we need to focus on the object they built – the master's *house*. There is so much emphasis on the word tools that we have missed the significance of the word *house*…Even the house as we know it today is not a place of coziness and warmth but a place of market value, privatization, and ego extension.

You can hang decorations in the master's house. You can spray slogans about freedom on its wall. You can create altars of equality in its gardens. But the master's house will still be a prison for everyone but the master himself.

When 'decolonising education' is about 'stockpiling examples of injustice yet will not make an explicit commitment to social justice' (Tuck and Wang, 2014, p. 223), it is 'dead.' It necessitates unpacking the tools and technologies that mystify the realities of colonial violence. Linda Tuhiwai Smith clearly told everyone that "the word itself, 'research,' is probably one of the dirtiest words in the indigenous world's vocabulary" (Smith, 2012, p. xi). Rethinking colonial understandings of academic *'Research'* requires living and engaging in *'Mesearch,'* persistently interrogating our own positionality, orientation and knowledge that has the pretension of universality and neutrality considering the needs of the communities we serve '*Wesearch'* (Douglas, 2017). Clelia's words carried an unmistakable weight of pain. I felt it cutting through my heart. It required an open heart and mind to appreciate it. You know better when you have had the privilege of learning from Clelia's teachings as part of the series and work, she leads as the Founder of SEEDS for Change. Clelia's words reminded me of my mother, Raina Usayi, who transitioned to glory. My mother used to throw a slipper at us to say, 'You know better,' reminding us of her daily teachings, and Clelia rebuking the use of colonial tools such as 'exploration,' saying, "*how much more exploration do we need to force ourselves to go through?*" My mother throwing the slipper was 'radical love.' Clelia saying, "I have been explored enough," was and is radical love. To learn that our 'decolonising education' book was already *dead* before it materialised was to face my vulnerability, a tender revelation that the idea we thought held the brilliance of transforming higher education practices and processes, did not. It was an experience that truly challenged our egos and confronted our attachment to the idea we felt carried transformative power. Following our meeting, two co-editors left the 'decolonising education' book. I wondered how it must have felt for Clelia to have the 'dead' book initiative dumped on her lap when she had already invested a lot. It was the depth of what this all meant that troubled me.

Clelia's words struck a chord and forged an unspoken bond. Accepting that our idea was already dead was not failure but a horizontal openness to confronting the difficulty of letting go of the *fading echoes of 'decolonising education.'* With a willingness and responsibility over my liberation, I embraced Clelia's invitation to '*crawl*' with her on the unconventional co-edited book 'Who are you without colonialism?.' This work is not for the likes, as she consistently speaks and writes about.

WHO ARE YOU WITHOUT COLONIALISM?

Inspired by Clelia's ancestors to connect us all and connect our ancestors through the unconventional call for papers, some of the contributors to this book have had *the privilege*, to learn from Clelia's SEEDS for Change teachings. They offer multivocal personal narratives in response to the question. To envision a world free from colonial oppression is to embrace the richness of our differences whilst acknowledging our shared humanity. This book invites readers to connect with these personal narratives, transcending physical and psychological borders that separate us, to chart a path towards a possible future as we confront the echoes of colonial legacy and shape a narrative that empowers us to ponder and contemplate "Who we are without colonialism."

> We are the rhythm of sacred dance,
> The language of the earth, in every trance,
> The knowledge of the mountains that ground us,
> How we create a path on a rock surface, *Dwala*.
>
> Through art and craft, our ancestors unite,
> Painting the canvas with colours so bright,
> With threads of liberation shining through,
> The digital media canvas of openness.

From the rainforests to desert islands,
We possess an unbreakable bond with the Mother Earth,
As the guardians of ancestral lands and knowledges,
Respectfully relating with more than human world,
Our hearts beat with rhythm.

No longer defined by imposed colonial divide,
Our voices join in solidarity,
Our veins flow stories of unbreachable trust and unity.

Embracing liberatory and horizontal openness to unconventional 'editorial' work allowed a process of deep listening and attuning respectfully and sensitively to the sacred work of all contributors to this book whilst being conscious of my positionality and orientation. Acknowledging that we experience this world differently and allowing multivocal offerings to co-exist and reinforce each other was fundamental to the unconventional 'editorial' process. This approach recognises that the sacred wisdom offered by each contributor is valuable to the collective pedagogies of liberation. The interconnectedness of our truths, realities and hope for a liberated present and future enriches this living book.

This is the opening note. She concludes it at the end.

REFERENCES

Douglas, T. (2017). My reasonable response: Activating research, mesearch, wesearch to build systems of healing. *Critical Education, 8*(2), 21–30. http://ojs.library.ubc.ca/index.php/criticaled/article/view/186223

Rodríguez, C. O. (2023). *Pedagogies of liberation teachings. SEEDS for change: Learning without boarders*. https://www.seedsforchange.ca/learning-without-borders

Lorde, A. (1984). *Sister outsider*. Penguin.

Ndhlovu-Gatsheni, S. (2017, September 26). Decolonising research methodology must include undoing its dirty history. *The Conversation*. https://theconversation.com/decolonising-research-methodology-must-include-undoing-its-dirty-history-83912

Salami, M. (2020). *Sensuous knowledge: A Black feminist approach for everyone*. Zed.

Smith, L. T. (2012). *Decolonizing methodologies* (2nd ed.). Zed Books.

Tuck, E., & Yang, K. W. (2014). R-Words: Refusing research. In D. Paris & M. T. Winn (Eds.), *Humanising research: Decolonising qualitative inquiry with youth and community*. Sage.

Chihera Shava Mhofu

Libation Offering to Ancestors

Faith Mkwesha

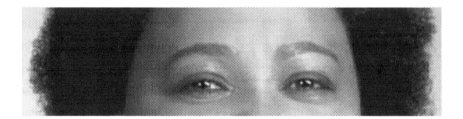

Libation, as practised by Africans, is the offering of drinks like water and brewed beer to Ancestral spirits in gratitude of blessings. In Zimbabwe we pour, *doro remasese* (traditional beer) mixed with snuff on the ground, while naming the Ancestors. We address them using the totem to invite their presence. Beer is poured to the Earth. The invocation process starts with the name of the last Ancestor to transition to the oldest asking them to present our gratitude and requests to *Mwari Musiki,* The One in Us.

The One in Us who is the Life Creative Energy Divine Force. In Shona Spirituality and Culture this Divine Life Force is not a human being. The libation ritual ceremony is performed when the traditional beer is placed inside a *pfuko* clay pot with a narrow neck with different decorations.

It is poured on the ground because we came from Mother Earth and to Her we return, as reflected in the ritual at funerals when we pick soil and throw it in the grave saying from the Earth we return;

Ivhu kuvhu.

I invite you to use different libation liquids you may use in your culture (water, wine, beer, milk, tea, coffee.
I invite you to pour the liquid in a container.
I invite you to pour the liquid on the soil.
I invite you to perform the libation for this book.
I invite you to present your libation prayer with Respect.
I invite you to meditate.
I invite you to contemplate.
I invite you to show up with solidarity which I begin with salutations to my own Ancestors.
I invite you to pour slowly drop-by-drop on the ground or container and read this libation with me, in community:

Salutations to Our Predecessors!

The bones that keep on rising until we are free!
Chihera, Mhofu, Hwata Shava Mupfakose, Mbuya NeHanda Charwe Nyakasikana svikiro of Shona People, leader of the First Chimurenga (first rebellion), Mhondoro Yenyika! (One of Royal National Spirits)!
Inspirer of the Second Chimurenga (Liberation Struggle) and The Third Chimurenga (Farm Invasions to take back Land).
To All Those who came before us;
Our Predecessors,
Those who perished in the Oceans,
Those Women who threw their children off the slavery ships,
Those who survived the perilous journeys and the inhuman labour in the plantations,
To the Ancestors who endured the dehumanisation of Settler Colonialism,
Those who lost their lives fighting for the land stolen by colonisers and land grabbers,
Those who fought to liberate the oppressed,
Those who organised resistance against domination and oppression!
We remember you; we honour you and salute you!

We call upon the elders in our lineages to pass on our gratitude to the Ancestors.
We invoke our biological, intellectual and Earthly Ancestors to present our heartfelt thank you to the Creative Force Mwari, the One in Us
who has blessed us with life, health and empowered us to create all the knowledge, while reclaiming indigenous wisdom presented in this book.

Thank you for the Visitations in Visions. Whispers, Dreams. Voices, Readings, Intuition and Tangling Feelings, Heritage! Without your inspiration, intellectual, spiritual, and emotional support this book would not have manifested into reality.
We appreciate your presence flowing in this book.

Chihera Shava Mhofu • 3

We thank The Spirit Mediums, Community Elders, Channelers, Messengers, Seekers, Teachers, Healers, Creators and Change Makers for the Knowledge in this book.
To the Contributors, may the elbows of all the Content Creators be oiled.
We pay homage to all the Contributors for availing selves to be channelers of wisdom and Knowledge presented here. We embrace the rich indigenous heritage.

We call upon the Ancestors of the readers and their descendants to engage with this diverse collection of work and comprehend the deeper meanings.
We implore settler descendants haunted by *Ngozi*, our avenging spirits for bodies, heads and cultural artifacts in your museums and vaults, whose ancestors inflicted so much pain, spilled human blood, caused death and generational trauma; ask your Colonial Ancestors to allow you, Settler descendant's readers to accept this collective offering.

In the spirit of Ubuntu, I am who I am in relation to others.
The African philosophy of Oneness,
We are Interconnected,
By our history,
By our humanity,
By one Living Earth,
By the environment,
By All there is.
We are interdependent.

We implore you and your capitalism!
Stop extractivism and destruction.
Stop racism and oppression.

Stop wars and death.
Stop colonising our minds.
We come from legitimate knowledges.
We are one humanity, one world.

May you end the circle of violence by acknowledging genocide of slavery and colonialism; appease the troubled souls by paying reparations and returning what is not yours to rightful owners. Thus, opening the way to the possibilities of reconciliation and healing.

May the life force in this Diverse Creation nourish our minds, souls, and hearts. Teach resilience, survival, compassion, and unconditional love for one another. Love symbolised by the co-creation we gift to everyone who will engage with this living book.

Faith Mkwesha Chihera Shava Mhofu. Kupira kuVadzimu vedu

Kupira kuVadzimu, sezvinoitwa muAfrika, kuchishandiswa zvinwiwa zvakaita semvura nedoro kumadzitateguru neMidzimu yedu tichitenda maropafadzo. MuZimbabwe tinodira doro remasese rakasanganiswa nefodya pasi, tichitaura neMadzitateguru. Doro rinodirwa Pasi. Tinotaura navo tichishandisa mutupo nezvidao zvavo tichitevedzera magwara avo ekuenda kunyika dzimu, tichitanga nanyakupedzisira kuenda neakatevera nemaendero avo kunyikadzimu. Tichivatenda nezvikomborero zvedu uye kukumbira kusvitsirwa zvichemo zvedu kuna Mwari Musiki Mukuru.

Uyo ari Matiri anova Musiki weHupenyu anemasimba akadzikadzika. MuChiShona cheMweya neTsika iye Mwari Samasimba weHupenyu Hunoraramisa haasi munhu kwete. Kupira kunoitwa nedoro rechinyakare remasese rinoiswa mukati mepfuko yevhu ine mutsipa mutete nekushongedzwa kwakasiyana siyana.

Doro rinodirwa pasi nokuti takabva kuna Mai vedu Ivhu, nokudaro kwaVari Kuvhu tinodzokera, sezvinoitwa mutsika dzedu pamariro patinononga ivhu torikanda muguva tichiti; "Ivhu kuvhu."

Ini ndinokukokai kuti mushandise zvinwiwa zvakasiyana-siyana zvaunoshandisa mutsika yako (mvura, waini, doro, mukaka, tii, kofi.)

Ndinokukokai kuti mudurure mvura mumudziyo.
Ndinokukokai kuti mudire mvura muvhu.
Ndinokukokai kuti mupe mupiro webhuku rino.
Ndinokukokai kuti mudire mupiro wekupira neRuremekedzo.
Ndinokukokai kuti mufungisise.
Ndinokukokai kuti muratidzire nekubatana kwandinotanga kuratidzira nekuteura kuMadzitateguru vangu.
Ndinokukokai imi kuti mudururire zvishoma nezvishoma muchidonhedza pasi kana mumudziyo

Muuye muverenge muteuro uyu neni, mukubatana kwedu:
Avo vakapararira mumagungwa eAtirandiki,
Vakadzi vakanda vana vavo kubva mungarava dzeuranda,
Avo vakazvikanda kunze mumvura,
Avo vakapukunyuka nzendo dzine njodzi uye basa rehuranda muminda,
Avo vakatsungirira hutsinye hwevapambi vepfuma uye vasveti veropa,
Avo vakarwira kusunungura vaidzvinyirirwa!

Tinokuremekedzi! Tinokurangarirai, Tinokukwazisai.

Tinodaidza midzimu yedu kuti vasvitse kutenda kwedu kuMadzitateguru edu naNyadenga. Tinokumbira madziteteguru edu ekuberekwa, enjere uye ePanyika kuti tiratidze kutenda kwedu kunobva pamwoyo kuna Simba reKusika Mwari, Uyo ari Matiri. akatikomborera nehupenyu, hutano uye akatipa simba rekugadzira ruzivo rwese, tichitorazve huchenjeri hwechivanhunetsika dzedu huri mubhuku rino.

Tinotenda nekushanyirwa kwese muZviono, Zvizeve-zeve, Zviroto, Manzwi, Kuverenga, Kukwenyawa, Nhaka Yedu, Manzwiro! Pasina tsigiro yenyu yehungwaru, yemweya uye nemupfungwa bhuku iri haringadai riripo. Tinotenda kuvepo kwenyu mubhuku rino.

Tinotenda Homwe, Masvikiro, Nhume, Vakuru vedu, Vanotsvaka, Vadzidzisi, Varapi, Varuki, uye Vanyori vemashoko ari mubhuku rino. Dai mazodzwa mafuta emagokora kuvanyori. Isu tinopa rukudzo kune mumwe nemumwe nekuda kwekuzviita homwe inosvikirwa nehuchenjeri uye ruzivo runomiriirwa pano. Tinombundikira nekutambira hupfumi hwenhaka yechivanhu uye kufunga kwakadzama kuri mubhuku rino.

Tinokoka midzimu yevaverengi kuti vawane makomborero akasiyana siyana ekunzwisisa zvakanyorwa. Tinokoka zvizvarwa zvevatorwa zvinotambudzwa neNgozi, dzemweya yedu yekutsividza kuti tiwane mitumbi, mabhonzo, misoro uye zviwanikwa neupfumi hwedu zviri mumamuziyamu enyu nemudzimba dzenyu; imi vane madzitateguru akarwadzisa zvakanyanya, vakateura ropa revanhu, vakakonzera rufu uye kushungurudzika kwezvizvarwa zvedu; kumbirai madzitateguru enyu echihupambepfumi kuti akubvumirei imi vaverengi

Kubudikidza nemweya weUnhu - ndiri zvandiri kubudikidza nevamwe.
Huzivi hweAfrica hweKubatana,
Isu takabatana,
Nenhoroondo yedu,
Nehunhu hwedu,
Nekurarama muNyika pamwe,
Nezvakatipoteredza,
Nezvose zviripo.
Isu tinokochekerana.

Tinokukumbira iwe uye kapitarizimu yako!
Rega ekistira tizimu uye kuparadza.
Rega rusaruraganda uye udzvanyiriri.
Rega hondo nerufu.
Rega kupamba pfungwa dzedu.
Tinobva muruzivo rwechokwadi.
Tiri vanhu vamwe, nyika imwe.

Dai mapedza ziyendanakuyenda remhirizhonga nekubvuma mhosva yehumhondi nehutapwa, nyaradzai mweya inodzungaira nekuripa nekudzosera zvamakapamba zvisiri zvenyu kuvaridzi vazvo. Ndiko kuti muvhure nzira yekuyanana uye kuporeswa.

Dai simba reupenyu riri muZvinyorwa Zvakasiyana-siyana izvi rapinda mupfungwa dzedu, mumweya uye mumwoyo yedu. Tidzidzisei kushinga, kurarama, tsitsi, uye rudo rusina magumo kune mumwe nemumwe. Rudo runofananidzirwa nemushandira pamwe wakaitwa watinopa kune wese achanzwisisa muono webhuku reupenyu iri.

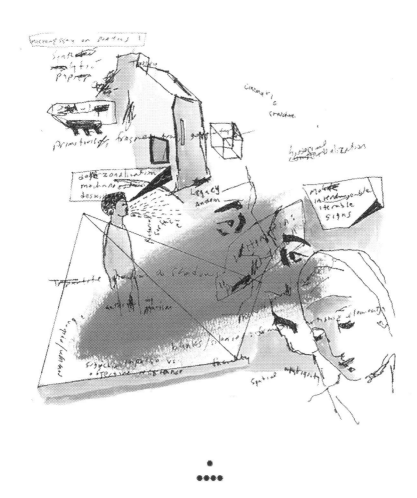

Octavio Quintanilla. A Micro-Essay on the "Micro-Essays on Poetics."

Micro-Essay on Poetics #1." 10"x10" Mixed media on linen finish paper.

..

I Am Who I Am

Pamela Lynn Chrisjohn

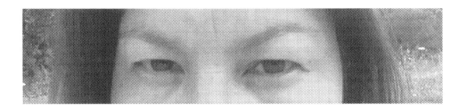

Before I was subjected to institutional learning, my introduction to this world was to observe land formations, animal habitats, seeing the colors of the sky, reading the stars, listening to bugs and the seasonal songs of birds, knowing when the wind changed direction, when hunting was good. I would watch the cycle of plants, gaze at the moon, lay on the grass, climb trees and feel various weather patterns...

I could read water before I could speak, mirrored puddles, lazy waves, misty rainfall, crashing lakes, diving waterfalls, old muddy creeks. My dad loved to cast a reel, he would also spearfish so our family would always find and follow the waterways wherever we travelled. He taught me in every environment I enter, I should be keenly aware of all my senses, especially to believe in my intuitive self-awareness.

At five years old, one of my earliest profound and truly scary memories is of my father telling me no one knows why we are here on Earth, and no one really knows exactly how we all spread out to different locations on the planet. Sure, he shared MANY theories and other creation stories throughout the years, however now, this was his introduction to what he said he was 100% sure of and I was told… "we", the Haudenosaunee (People of the Longhouse), are to always base our decisions on those not yet born, to consider the effects of our choices seven generations into the future.

I was completely dumbfounded when my dad asked me to imagine the children who would be coming into the world many years from our pre-school conversation and long after he was gone. He said kids like me would be wondering about the world, and then he seriously asked me how I would care for them. "Wait, gone?" Care for whaaat!?" Well, years later, I have been blessed to come across so many of those beautiful Onkwehonwe spirits we spoke of so many years ago. Rest well Dad, Kennard "Kenny" Anthony Chrisjohn.

Gratitude to all the ancestors before us is important for the Haudenosaunee. The recognition of those who have left behind the gift of knowledge and the many tools imperative to our survival on our mother earth is a large part of our ceremonial practice.

The original five nations of the Haudenosaunee Confederacy (later to include Tuscarora) are the only known league of nations on this planet who have truly achieved peace after ruthlessly waring for many years. Remarkably more than 2000 years later, "The Great Law of Peace" is still maintained within our distinct nations' territories. It is each of our duty to uphold the peace.

I have been taught that my number one responsibility is to keep a good mind and peace (within). When we greet one another, the question is asked; "is the peace with you?" the second is, "which clay are you from" otherwise asking one's name, clan family, nationhood, and land base/territory.

As I grew, my bedtime stories became more of geographical, historical, and political recounts of the formation of the various nations on the North and South American continents. Our Haudenosaunee Confederacy predates contact by more than 1400 years and is still going strong. We have our creation stories and still maintain the original instructions from the creator in our longhouse ceremonial practices. Along with our traditional stories, I was informed of imperialism and racism, somehow, the struggles of the antagonists in my father's stories would include many frustrating injustices.

My entire nation views themselves as sovereign people, completely separate from Canada and the United States. Being from this strong Oneida lineage, with my father, aunts, cousins, great grandparents being titleholders, I am to embrace my community and never to abandon my responsibilities. Learning my ABC's meant I must reject "a"ssimilation, brutality and colonialism.

Mentors, family, teachers, elders, and medicine people have graciously and humbly shared cultural knowledge. I know what my responsibilities are as a matriarch. I must always protect the land (our mother), and I will teach my daughters to do the same. My dad used to say, "Every day is a good day to die, for the land, for what is right, for my grandchildren, my family, my clan, my nation, and my Haudenosaunee Confederacy, for the people."

Coming from a matriarchal society the life-giver is held in high regard, our words are to be respectfully thoughtful and peaceful. After months of giving cultural knowledge to students of various levels in online webinars and lectures, I now know who it is I must teach… my children, the children of my community, the children of the confederacy, indigenous children, they are the only people I want to hand my knowledge over to.

Everything I now create is for those yet to be born…

Octavio Quintanilla. A Micro-Essay on the "Micro-Essays on Poetics."

Micro-Essay on Poetics #2." 10"x10" Mixed media on linen finish paper.

•••

Dai pasina hupambepfumi ndiri ani?

Josephine Gabi

A deep realisation weighs upon me as I sit here contemplating the intricate dynamics of my academic pursuit and ancestral reverence. Academia has riddled me with a unique paradox. I have been writing in English, a language that carries a colonial view of the world tinged with a set of ideologies. The ghost of linguistic imperialism continues to linger in my every utterance of this colonial tongue. It is a language my mother, Raina Usayi, who nurtured me with all her love and care, cannot fully comprehend. I imagine how fascinating and wondrous it must have been for her watching me, as a child; learn to speak my first words in Shona Zezuru, my mother tongue, during the British colonial rule. Colonial intricacies of the approval process within academia and adhering to these protocols put me in a conflicting juxtaposition: I am entangled in a web of complexity. Writing from the academic tower, I cannot help but ponder my intentions with my continued engagement in English. How much longer do I want to continue perpetuating harm, erasing the histories and ignoring the living Knowledges and ways of being of my Shona Zezuru community in Bare, Chiweshe in Zimbabwe by shrouding it in the obscurity of linguistic imperialism and academic jargon? I have no spiritual and emotional connection to English. I think in Shona and translate to English. I sometimes encounter the untranslatability of the Shona language where some words do not mean the same thing in English. It is a painful dance between languages.

To my fellow diaspora who continue to be hamstrung by the remnants of colonialism, I say it is crucial to recognise the harm caused by perpetuating the toxicity of colonial logics that subjugates our mother tongues and cultures. By choosing not to speak our languages, write in our languages and fail to pass them on to our children, we inadvertently contribute to the erasure of our cultural identities and the identity of others. Such intentional neglect perpetuates the inferiorisation of who we are. With a conscious anticipation of the possibilities ahead, in my writing below, I share who I am without colonialism in my mother tongue, the Shona Zezuru language from Zimbabwe—a methodology and mentorship path through the teachings of Dr. Clelia O. Rodríguez. Deceiving others or myself about my intentions would only lead to a false sense of purpose of my writing. Like Dylan Robinson, I write "for a readership yet to come, for future generations of fluent [Shona] readers and speakers, of which there are currently few" (Robinson, 2020:25). With this Pedagogy framed as Liberation from linguistic bondage, an intentional act to 'decolonise my mind' (Ngugi Wa Thiongo), I write in Shona with pride as a form of refusal and resistance of the lingering effects of colonialism and also to preserve my heritage for my children. If you do not understand Shona, as Dr. Rodríguez eloquently articulates when she is teaching "it is not for your comprehension. Not everything is written to cater to everyone's sensibilities." You are not the audience. Resist the urge to translate and allow pluriversal forms of expression to co-exist whilst understanding that they may not meet each other in full embrace. Still, in humility, we appreciate the sanctity of linguistic diversity that enriches our shared experience. Beyond what words on a page might do, I am responsible for my liberation and accountable for what I do, as I simultaneously inhabit two linguistic worlds.

DAI PASINA HUPAMBEPFUMI NDIRI ANI?

Ndiri mwana wekuAfrika. Nhaka uye tsika nemagariro angu zvinodarika ruvara rweganda rangu. Kungozivikanwa se'mutema' kukoshe sa zvisina maturo, nekuti kukosha kwangu kunodarika ruvara rweganda rangu, kukosha kwangu kwechokwadi kunobva muhunhu hwangu nechimiro changu. Maungira emiganhu yakachekwa nevapambepfumi yakatikanganisa pfungwa nokadyara mhodzi yerusarura, kupatsanura vanhu vamwe nenyika dzakaita seZimbabwe, Zambia, South Africa, Mozambique, neUganda kunyangwe nanhasi. Ini ndinozvisunungura nemaune kubva mukupatsanurwa patsanurwa uku, ndinosarudza kuzendamira kuhunhu netsika dzedzinza rangu nekuva mugari wenyika. Ini ndinobva kuMashonaland

Central, kuBare chaiko kuChiweshe, dunhu kwaSabhuku Makope kunova kwakavigwa rukuvhute rwangu rwakachererwa muvhu reNyika yamai vangu. Ndiri mwana wevhu. Ndine chisungano nenyika yamadzitateguru angu chisingaputswe nekuganhurwa ganurwa asi chinotekeshera nepasi. Ini ndiri mumwe nenyika ine ivhu rakavigwa rukuvhute rwangu, zvirimwa, zvimerwa, zvinomiririra chisungano chedu chekupindana pindana, kubatana, kuremekedza neutariri. Ini ndiri mugari anoshingaira shingaira, muchengeti, ane mutoro wekuchengetedza uye kukoshesa nharaunda yakaberekwa ikakurira nekuvigwa madzitateguru angu. Rurimi rwakakononzverwa rwandinotaura rwaamai vangu ChiShona chemaZezuru emuZimbabwe. Handirasike, kana kubiwa, ndakafanana neverudzi rwangu—Ndiri muera Soko Mukanya. Vana makwira miti, vanochenjenza maoko nekuchenjera pfungwa.

    Ndakakwana. Ruvara rweganda rangu haruratidzi kukosha kwangu semunhu. Kuti ndini ani hakubve 'pahutema,' kundidzikisira kuruvara rweganda rangu. Ruvara rweganda rangu haruratidzi kukosha kwangu; asi, ndinobvumwa uye ndinoremekedzwa semunhu, ndinoyemurwa nekudzika kwehunhu hwangu, kupenya kwematarenda angu, uye kubatsira kwandinoita pasirese. Kunzi uri munhu zvinobva pamagariro ako nevamwe nezvese zvisikwa: kuve nemoyo munyoro, netsitsi, kukudza. Ruremekedzo nechiremerera. Kutambira vanhu vese inzira yehupenyu inopemberera kupfuma kwenhaka yangu yeAfrica, tsika, hunhu. uye zvitendero zvakatichengeta kwemazana emakore. Kunzi munhu, kuve nehunhu hunomhanya nemutsinga dzangu. Hunhu hwakadzama zvekunzwisisa kuti munhu munhu kuburikidza nevamwe, munhu anokoshesa mutserendende mukugarisana nevamwe pasina mhirizhonga nemakakatanwa. Hunhu chisimbiso chehumunhu uye kucherechedzwa kwehumunhu hwevamwe vanhu, nekudaro ndinovaka hukama hwechokwadi, hune huremekedzo mekunzwisisana. Segwara rekurarama zvine ungwaru muukama, izvi zvinounza rukudzo neyemuro. kwete kutsvaga kutsiva asi kuyanana. Nokuti ini ndinogona kunzi handisi munhu' kana hunhu hwangu husina kunaka uye hwakafumuka, semuenzaniso, kana ndikapfuura munhu ndisina kumumhoresa ini ndichiziva kuti kumhoresa munhu kubvuma humunhu hwake ndinenge ndisina kuratidza hunhu. Nekudaro ndinenge ndaita zvisingataridzira ndinenge ndisina kuratidza hunhu. Nekudaro ndinenge ndaita zvisingatarisirwe kuti munhu anehunhu angaite. Dzimwe nguva unonzwa vakuru vachitsiura kuti hauna kukwana kana kuti urimbwa yemunhu. Kuvevanhu kwedu kuzviona mune vamwe kuchisimbiswa nekubatana uye kudyidzana kwedu. Tichikwazisana tinoti, makadii? Mhinduro inoti 'Ndakasimba kana makadiiwo'. Zvoreva kuti kusimba kwangu kunovepo kana iwe wakasimbawo, kana iwe usiri kunzwa zvakanaka uri kurwara zvinoreva kuti iniwo handisi kunzwa zvakanaka. Handisi munhu ndega, anozvimirira ega, ndinosunganidzwa neumwe munhu. Nokudaro chinorwadza umwe munhu chinondirwadzawo. Kuzivikanwa kwangu kunosanganisira nyaya, nhoroondo, zvisikwa, tsika nemagariro uye zviitiko zvakapfuura nemuzvizvarwa zvakapfuura kana kuti madzitateguru angu. Nemufaro ndichizvikudza ndinombundira rungano rwekubatana kwedu kuti kuenderere mberi mupasi rese ririkuchinja, tinopemberera uye tinoratidzira huwandu hwehumunhu hwedu, ruvara rwedu ruchipa humboo hwemavara eganda redu anoshongedza jira rehupenyu hwedu sechiratidzo chemakumi ezviuru tichirarama mararamiro ehukama hwakadzama.

Ndinopemberera uye ndinotambira nhaka yangu yetsika neunhu ndisingatyi kusarurwa; Ini ndinouya sezvandiri nebvudzi rangu reAfro kana tsine, korona yangu, chiratidzo cherunako rwangu chinobudisa pachena chinzvimbo changu munharaunda. Hapana mushonga wekupisa bvudzi rangu kuti riti tsepete nemusoro, kurishandura zvinodiwa nevanamazvikokota vemakambani emabasa, kuita zvinonzi zvakanaka uye zvinechimiro chinodiwa nekuremekedzwa munharaunda yese. Makambani kana maindasitiri ebvudzi retsine kana afro haite mari yakawanda nekugadzira bvudzi remadzimai matema zvakasiyana nemagadziriro emadzitateguru edu kuti vawane basa nemari. Pasina upambepfumi tingadai tisina kurwadziswa kusingayereki uye kutambura kwakaiswa patiri tose, fungidziro inotyisa inemutinhimira kuburikidza nekuziva kwedu pamwechete; nhaka yekushandiswa, udzvanyiriri, uye kuuraya tsika, mitauro uye kudzima madzidziro kunokonzerwa nemafungiro ehupambepfumi akambandidzirwa patiri nanhasi uno, kuumba kusaenzana kwemagariro ehupfumi uye kuenderera mberi kwehurongwa hwekudzvanyirira. Maronda akakonzerwa nehupambepfumi anodzika zvakadzama, uye tinofanira kurwisana nemagumisiro ekutambudzika kwemarudzi akawanda kuchiri kuitika muna 2023. Mavanga enguva yerima iyi akasiya zvakawanda panhoroondo dzedu, ruzivo rwezvehupenyu uye chokwadi chemamiriro ezvinhu. Mubvunzo unogara uripo wokuti, 'Unobva kupi?' unongoramba uripo setsine (blackjack), kwose kwandinoenda. Kutaura kuti unobva kuManchester pano neapo kunokoka mubvunzo unotevera, 'Ndiri kureva kwawakabva pekutanga?' Uyu mubvunzo unoratidzika kunge usina mhosva asi unochera zvakadzama. Mubvunzo iwoyu unonetsa nekushamisa vana vangu vakaberekerwa munyika ino. Pasina upambepfumi ndinomira ndichidada, ndisingaremerwi nechikonzero chekutaura kwandakabva. Ndiri mugari wepasi rose. Isu tose tiri vagari vepasi rose!

Pandinofunga nezvenhaka yeupambepfumi ndinoyeuchidzwa izwi rekuti 'Mutema' rinoreva shanduko, rinoshanda senzvimbo yekuronga kurwisa mauto ehupambepfumi anoda kurerutsa hupenyu hwedu. Inotungidza murazvo wegungano rekubatana kunopisa zvakajeka kunyangwe munguva dzakasviba kana dzakaoma. Ẹniọlá Ànúolúwapọ́ Ṣóyẹmí, anotiyeuchidza kuti kutaura nezverudzi hakufanire kunge kuri kuenzanisa 'mavanga' edu kana kuona kuti hutema hwaani 'hwakasvibisisa' kana kuti hunorwadza sezvo izvi zvichiita kuti simba rehupambepfumi rirebe ihwo huchifanira kubviswa. Pane kudaro, tinofanira kutaura nezverudzi kuti titorezve nhoroondo dzedu, tichiisa huvanhu pamberi uye nekumira pachokwadi kuti tisu vanhu vacho munharaunda. Ndinozvipira zvisingazunungutki kuumba ramangwana risina zvisaririrwa zvepfungwa dzeupambepfumi, zvirasirwe kune musarirwa wezvinorwadza zvenhoroondo—inoyeuchidza chibayamwoyo chekubatana kwedu pamwe chete nezvishuvo zvepasi rakaenzana. Kubvuma uye kunzwisisa maronda asingapori uye nokurwadza kwawo kwakakosha pakumutsa tsitsi, nekukuridzira remangwana rakavakwa nekuyananisa uye kuremekedzana. Tinogona kuedza kugadzirisa zvakakanganisika munguva yakapfuura inosuwisa munhoroondo yedu tese kuburikidza nekubvuma nemoyo wose zvakaitika zvinozivikanwa nekuunza kuyanana. Pamwechete, tinogona kuvhura nzira yekuenda mberi kune ramangwana rakajeka, iro rinokurudzirwa nechiedza chetariro kuzvizvarwa zvichauya.

REFERENCES

Ngũgĩ wa Thiong'o. (1986). *Decolonising the mind: The politics of language in African literature*. Heinemann.

Robinson, D. (2020). *Hungry listening: Resonant theory for indigenous sound studies*. University of Minnesota Press.

Rodríguez, C. O. (2023). *Pedagogies of liberation-based teachings*. SEEDS for Change: Learning Without Borders. https://www.seedsforchange.ca/learning-without-borders

Ṣóyẹmí, E. A. (2019, May 17) Are Nigerians 'Black' Enough to Talk About Race?: Re-imagining the Discourse on Race. *The Republic*. https://republic.com.ng/april-may-2019/nigerians-black-race/

Octavio Quintanilla. A Micro-Essay on the "Micro-Essays on Poetics."
Micro-Essay on Poetics #3." 10"x10" Mixed media on linen finish paper.

Land/Home Dreaming

Glenda Mejía

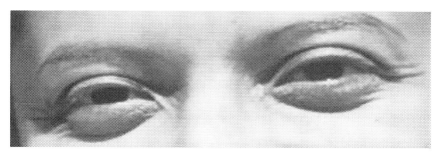

Without colonialism
I'm naked, estoy desnuda.
I feel land, siento mi tierra.
I dream my land, sueño con mi tierra.
I dig mis talones into a black, moist, fertile land.
Cuando entierro mis talones, un dolor fuerte corre por mis piernas,
por todo mi ser
y de pronto el dolor se va,
me siento libre,
me siento desnuda,
me siento tranquila,
agua corre por mi cuerpo.
My dreams remind me to anchor to land,
to connect my body to land and water.

I see water, I feel water.
My dreams remind me que soy agua.
My dreams remind me to connect to my ancestors,
to heal myself,
to forgive myself,
remind me to disfrutar de mi desnudez y mis deseos.
In my dreams I see colour,
I see a mi abuelita Berta,
I see su sonrisa.
I close my eyes and I see myself at 5 years old closing her eyes the day she died.
I close my eyes and
I see myself singing to her, believing that with my song, her pain will go away.
Le canto when her uterus is bleeding and eaten by cancer.
She smiles saying, that my song is medicine.
I feel her, I feel her, I feel her.
Mis ojos se llenan de agua al sentir a mi abuelita.
Agua corre en mi cuerpo, siento su tristeza,
sus dolores,
sus vergüenzas.
Agua corre sobre mi cuerpo para sanar mis heridas,
mis dolores,
mi vientre.
I feel her, I feel her, I feel her.

Embroideries. This fabric is 29 cm wide, 15.5 cm and is part of another complimentary piece that follows on the next page. They are interconnected. I did do both, an embroidery and a painting of shared aquatic paths. The embroidery one is because my grandmother *Águila* was a seamstress. My grandfather, who I only saw once from afar, was a painter. I learned that he used to paint on oil and canvas. As part of the infinite ways to answer the question, Who are you without colonialism?, I share two teachings: To be aware of my feelings when I am learning because it makes me want to do things I had never done before and to be patient. Before I started the second piece, I waited. I left the rest, just as it was . . . I felt every stitch. It took me hours, days, months . . . I returned to it when my body asked me to. When I was making the parts that represent the land and legs I cried, OMG how I cried! When I did the arteries, I felt pleasure in my belly. When I was stitching the water, I was stuck thinking too much about how to translate my idea I then removed all the stiches, changed the stiches and colour, and I just let it flow, like aguas libres. Then I stopped.

When I finished it, something inside me pushed me to make a painting of the same dream and I did. This process was calm and fun, combining colours and finding the ones I felt and called me.

When I looked back at the painting, the colours remind me of where I come from and where I am. Two lands that, dos tierras, although far away from each other, are close to me, and I call them both home.

Land/Home Dreaming • 21

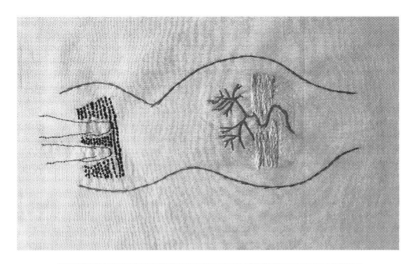

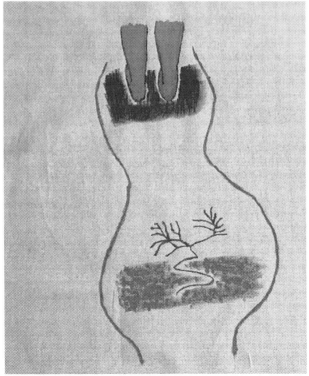

Entre dos lands. This is the complimentary painting to *Embroideries.* It is 13 cm wide; 27 long. Entre dos lands. When I sketched the embryo, I felt connected to my abuelita.

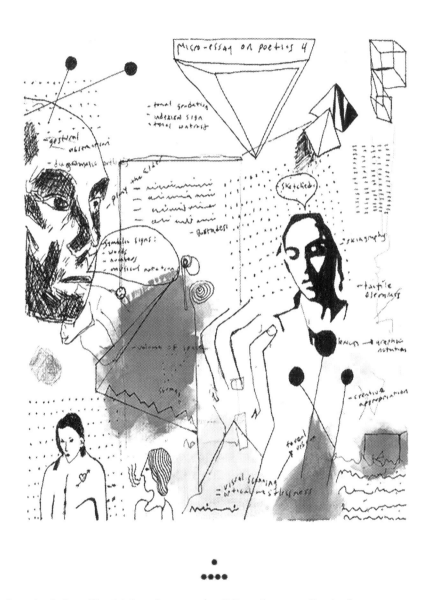

Octavio Quintanilla. A Micro-Essay on the "Micro-Essays on Poetics."
Micro-Essay on Poetics #4." 10"x10" Mixed media on linen finish paper.

The Night I Fell Into the Stars

Mary Chakasim

I walked to the riverbank along the Moose River in front of Moosonee in the dark. I sat down on the grass. The sandbar was gone. The full moon was out, its light reflecting on the water.

Silence.

It was late enough that there wasn't a single freighter canoe taxi out on the water. No cars on the road behind me. No one walking home from the dance.

I looked up and down the length of Charles Island across the river from me. One lone campfire was burning. I tried to imagine the smell of the wood burning. I thought of my favourite thing—bannock with raisins cooked on an ah-pwah-nah-tik. I imagined the sound of the fire crackling as it began to die down for the night.

I wondered who was there. Was that someone sitting and looking back at me? How loud would I need to speak to say hello? Voices are magnified at night.

I looked up at the moon and saw Chakabesh with his pail and a wooden spoon. I wondered who else was looking at the moon at this exact moment. Where are they? Do I know them? Will I meet them one day?

Such a clear beautiful night. The skin on my face was getting clammy in the cool air.

I looked up at the ocean of stars. Oh-chay-kah-dahk's large figure in the sky. Is there anyone out there staring back at me? I suddenly felt myself starting to shrink. Smaller and smaller. How insignificant I am in the universe. I grew tired in my soul. I was already 17 and hadn't served any purpose yet. I hadn't helped anyone. And I was about to leave home. Would I ever come back?

I don't want to go.

I don't want to go on.

I was lying on my back and felt a full body hug from the earth and the air. A deep, soothing voice from everywhere at once said "look up at those stars… if they felt the way you do, the sky would be dark".

I fell into the stars.

****

No earth below me, no sky above me. Floating in time and space, conscious only of my upper body, my lower half wading in the pool of the universe, the pool of the void.

Breathtaking, deep purple and blue, peace and calm. Tranquillity. I watched shooting stars all around me. My eyes moved in slow motion. Everything in this void all at once and nowhere to be seen.

I went to the meeting place of all souls.

Stars, the milky way, and planets filling the distance between you and me. Mesmerizing, dazzling sparkles of light in a dark deep blue sea of knowledge, fate and consciousness…

Infinite. The unknowable from all time in one place.

I am awestruck for the first time. Such joy. Such power. The miracle of its existence is undeniable and profound. I can see and hear and feel and breathe without a form or vehicle encasing or containing "me."

So vast and yet it was a part of me.

So vast and free and limitless. Still somehow, a vacuum, a limitless chamber with a cool unmoving breeze I felt on the skin of my arms and neck and face, though these parts of me were not there. All opposites we have created exist at once. Each thought echoed out loud though not heard by anyone. Each thought melding into the purpose of all in the meeting place.

I went to the meeting place of all souls that night.

To be reminded of the destiny I promised to live.

I noticed the sound of a seeseekwahn somewhere in the distance.

Koosh koosh koosh. The sound heard at creation, my grandmother, my mama, nookum, had told me.

Koosh koosh koosh. Where am I?

Several large, upright, rectangular thin screens of liquid silver morphed into existence one after another in a line to my distant right.

One by one, each bigger than life screen, racing towards me, then colliding with my essence to give me a window into that world. Merging with my awareness so I could see into that moment.

…Where I watched you and me in the specks of time, space, and knowledge allowable in each moment. You held my temple to yours. Pressure roaring in my ears. Images flashing through my mind like the individual frames of an old time movie film reel, at top speed. The bright liquid silver blocking out the view of everything around us. *koosh koosh koosh koosh*

Our souls trapped, separated, and unable to reach each other. Deep knowing and certainty. The meeting place…the void, rips me from the scene and freezes my grandfather's image to the surface of the liquid silver screen.

Koosh koosh koosh

No amount of time would have ever been enough; did I get what you tried to give to me?

In a fierce sudden movement, the silver screen topples over backwards, beginning its irreversible ferocious descent into the knowing, bottom over top, again and again, faster and faster until it is suddenly out of sight. My experience waited to hear the inevitable shatter of the screen—a million shards of mirrored glass shooting out into the meeting place of all souls—a shatter I never hear.

****

The energy and love released by the finality of the lostness of the scene reformed and reconfigured at warp speed to bring on the next reality and possess the next silver screen while the blow of the sudden deep grief from the first scene knocked me to my knowing knees.

I lost my grandfather. Again.

The next screen of liquid silver plummets towards me and breaks the barrier for my essence to see what once was but was never permitted to be…such love, connection and "meant to be"… again the scene raced away in a powerful backward somersault—not enough time to grab hold of the scene of you and me.

Energy ripped out of me, down on my knowing knees. Hit by new grief for what was taken from me and yet had never been and was not to be.

Another scene brought to me… Little ones! One, two, three?!

Bursting with first true love as I watched myself holding one little on my knees, another little on my chest, sleeping peacefully. I held her and kissed the top of her head as we walked silently in peace and calm, my hand in yours as you walked ahead of me carrying the third; we crossed a paved street covered in colourful but dry leaves that crinkled under our feet. A different man from reality.

One kiss, two, and three before laying down to sleep.

I suddenly remembered this scene is not "here" and "now". Can I will myself to stay in this scene? What do I do? I want to stay with my three little girls. Dread and panic flooded my being. This scene too would be hurled into the void. I needed to hang on but didn't know how. The void was coming for this liquid silver screen. I felt the scene start to tremble and shake. I flexed my essence and held on with every iota of energy allocated to "me." The void shook me loose; I bounced out of the world of silver like I was hit by a truck. My heart ripped out, I screamed a scream I never want to know in the here and now. My soul begged "pleeeease. My babies!" The void calmly but forcefully took the scene from me.

Inconsolable grief brought me to my knowing knees. Sobbing, I can't breathe. Exhausted and no longer wishing to be and yet I feared I was to exist for all eternity. My children I never knew. Their images trapped on that screen of silver yanked from my reach, spiralling into the knowing. I watched them plummeting into the universe, farther and farther away from me. Could I will them back? "I must!"

****

I got up off my knees that I couldn't see. I reached and strained and fought. I was held back by something unseen, like I was leaning over the side of a boat caught in a vicious storm. My rage and emotions, from all time, spinning like a hurricane. Faster and faster as the image of my babies taken from me faded into the pool.

Vanished.

With each breath I was able to take, I screamed "What is this?!"

"Why are you doing this to me?"

I screamed into the void. "What have I ever done?!"

"Where can I be?" "What can I do for you to bring them back to me?"

The void communicates these were times that couldn't be but were, in the screens of silver.

Couldn't be at 25 and 50, 32 and 57, 36 and 61, 40 and 65. 45 and 70 almost there. 48 and 73 crazy? "But now it will work," I'm told.

****

I went to the meeting place of all souls one night.

The Time Is Here.

Such pain and heartache and finality to see all that I lost, though it never was. Such deep love, the same in every scene. All together in totality unbreakable.

Each scene had not come to be because of some fatal shortcoming. One short step. One insignificant plan changed. Slideshows through space of all the times that never were, but should have been. One last minute decision disrupting what had been intended by our contract. Glances of happy moments we somehow shared but never had.

Contradiction.

The Time Is Here.

Wisdom in the meeting place makes me believe some people in our lives are there as fillers to take up space and occupy time while we wait for the stars to align, leading us to the destiny we vowed to live. The destinies in the screens of liquid silver… opportunities to fulfil our commitment to return.

The void showed me happiness I was able to feel despite a broken heart and shredded soul. So beautiful. To all the powers that be… "thank you for helping me."

So, why so long? Did free will cause this delay? Did your rationality or sense of duty prolong the wait here in this world? Should you have listened to your heart? Did you ever hear me?

Or.

Had I been afraid to start this life? The commitment was made, the contract signed. Did I not want to leave you? Had I wanted to stay a little longer with you in the meeting place of souls before coming to this world?

****

Our souls connected for all time and again for all time;
kahkekay meena kahkekay;
forever plus forever.

****

Did I watch you leave the meeting place of all souls to fulfil this destiny, unable to follow you? Did you rush too eager too fast into our future? Did you not hear me ask you to wait?

The mother I chose was not yet ready. I lost my children before they could even be. The channel was unable to flow. The door never opened. Because as time passed, 3 little souls had chosen me. To be. Their channel flowed and the door opened.

Their existence is in now, promising I will never know that agony. These three little souls, my loss of them I would never survive. Lead the way. She will fight back. Share. My soul mates.

I was their path in for the purpose they have… they found me despite the liquid silver mirrors of time, that should have been but weren't, because you jumped too soon. Their essences maybe re-formed and reconfigured to be with me, in now, from that time that was but couldn't be.

****

Why did I not come? Did I not believe you would meet me here? Did you have more faith? Did I choose to come too late? Had you sensed when I had finally arrived? Did I jump into this world for you because I knew you needed me?

The Time Is Here.

I tell you of fillers shared by the wisdom in the meeting space of all souls. You ask if you are a filler for me, just occupying time and space. I know you are not. I was shown you are not. Of that I am absolutely certain.

I tell you of fillers shared by the wisdom in the meeting space of all souls and you ask what if I am a filler for you. A thought I had never had. "What if I am"? The thought made me cry. You act as though I lie.

The Time Is Here.

We finally found each other. Our now is the last scene in the slideshow through space. There are no other mirrors of images plummeting through the universe. What does that mean? Maybe, what I am, really does remain to be seen. The thought made me cry.

Would the void have shown me this final scene if I am a filler? The possibility makes my heart ache. The same agony when my children I never knew were taken from me.

What if the passage of time changed my role from its original purpose? You jumped too soon!

What if *time is here* means this IS the last and final chance to reconnect before we meld into the meeting place of all souls? With the same deep oneness of the void. Totally unbreakable.

Except by destiny?

******

I finally jumped. I found my way by going home. I met you in that house. I took off my coat, set it down and made my way up the stairs to join you. "You made it!" you said in surprise and hugged and held me tight. In truth, I know you recognized me long ago but had never even said hello.

Maybe I should have jumped and followed you immediately. Maybe you should have looked back. Always moving too fast for me. If you rush ahead again now, before me, in this time and space, will I wait as long to go to you in the meeting place of all souls? Our contract is broken. Actually, now, this is truly a gift to me.

I look away from the screen of liquid silver. "I know him", I said to the void.

******

The Mystery, at risk once more. Something so surely meant for him and me. So hard to mend time and time again. My words spoken out loud echo and bounce off jagged rock walls in a dark valley I can't see. Why won't he hear me?

In my shoes, he will never be. The ultimate test he delivers to me repeated and repeatedly. Forgetting the underlying constant thread of tested patience laying at the foundation of all we have ever been in this world… this time.

fraying,

slowly snapping under the weight of this reality, the manifestation of Mystery delayed by earthly traps and man-made rules and bindings, so unnecessary, wasting our time day after day after day after day…

"Plans are in place", he says, yet shares these with no one who needs to know; the unfairness of that, digging into my soul—there is at least ONE who should know because living and planning and expectations will change. Actions never match words.

Selfish? It is said I am. Do I not share plans already made? Selfish.

Clearer than anything else ever before me. Clear clean crisp and sharp as the sound of a heavy teardrop landing on the thin mirror top surface of a cold lake. Too impulsive, unreliable, untrustworthy, cowardly. Narcissistic. Self-centred. The opposite of what you make sure the world sees.

The sadness of Mystery, sadness for me; its inevitability ignored and denied. Because it took too long to find me. The last lost opportunities holding children now kept hostage from me; ultimate arrogance, here, forcing their souls to find another way to me because of your choice not to act at the time they grew.

The pain and heartbreak breaching the surface intermittently like memories of loves lost to death.

The path to these souls I did not see.

The mystery was cruel to me though the path may not have been ruined by me. "Was he the one who should have acted then; did his waiting and 'planning' destroy my chance to be with them?" I asked the void.

The waiting, though Mystery has been shown to me. We wait, again.

When I think of foregoing that scene in the screen of liquid silver, the turmoil builds, knowing Mystery wants to fulfil its destiny. My frayed rope of patience is now only a thread.

The time was never right.

Too soon, too young to participate.

Too soon, too young to articulate

Too soon, too young to cooperate.

Too soon, too young to appreciate. Now time has caught up.

The Mystery spoke the words 'time is here.' How much time must pass before the Mystery leaves me?

That door is closed in the future.

******

"I know him." I speak to the void. "It's too late. He vanished into the darkness at the darkest time. When he next jumps time, I can't go with him. Three souls found me in my time despite him. I can't go." I now could not, would not, ever let it be.

At that, I felt finality.

Of that, I know isolation.

I felt the part of soul apportioned to me begin to shatter into shards of glass. Cushioned by the fact I had three most important portions of soul to be with me.

******

I hear the seeseekwahn again, from a distance but louder now –
KOOSH KOOSH KOOSH KOOSH.
Closer and closer.

A larger, thicker mirror of liquid silver moves deliberately towards me, bringing me comfort, acceptance and pure love. Coming to my aid. It makes me understand the purpose. And that the loss was truly not mine. My awareness joins the mirror and the show starts to play.

The seeseekwahn softer now, koosh koosh koosh.

I see myself at 6 years old walking in on my grandfather with his friend giving him a brush cut, in the back porch, with clippers. I hear my mother, aunts, and grandmother in the kitchen of the house. It's a beautiful summer day and I long to be back there. In response to something his friend said, Baba chuckles and says "our grandchildren are our secret weapons."

"What do you mean, Baba?", I ask the wall of silver. "What happened, Baba?"

The scene freezes and Baba looks up at me!

Startled that he could hear me, I repeat, "What happened, Baba?" I could feel his happiness at seeing me in the space around him; aware that he could not reach out to grab me and hug me to welcome me home, in tears, like he did every time I came home from school for the holidays, in the future? In the past? In the future? Where am I? Aware that he needed to talk. That he needed to talk right now. He looked at the 6 year old me frozen in the frame as he answered my question...

The machine took our land. It took our food.
The machine took our water.
The machine took our homes.
The machine took our pasts and our futures as they were meant to be.
The machine took our minds and our knowing of manitou.
And the machine took our tongues. Then...
they came for the children.

The Night I Fell Into the Stars • 31

I felt horror and dread.
Koosh koosh koosh…

They took our children to keep themselves safe from war.
They made our children hate their own thoughts, their homes, their own kin.

Images of black spruce trees, snow covered ground, large clumps of snowflakes lazily falling from the sky, and sparkling lakes and rivers, geese in flight, bright sunshine, morphed and melded into one another all around me as Baba answered me, while we watched the freeze frame of time, back when I was six, while everyone in the house talked and laughed quietly in the background. The seeseekwahn still shaking koosh, koosh, koosh…

They made our children hate and ridicule our ways.
They made them hate their own skin.
They took their tongues so that they would never be able to hear.
So that they'd never hear our stories from the time of first light.
They'd be left only with the talking paper that lies about what is true.

"What can I do?!," I blurted out, my voice echoing as if out on open land by a riverbank, dark, late at night.
"Stay," he said.

The shame is dying. It will soon be gone.
Taking the tongues of our grandchildren saved them from war as they imprisoned nature with pens.

(koosh koosh koosh)

Our children had no defence against them.
Our children had no protection from them.
They took our children's tongues, minds, bodies, and souls to do with as they wished.
Our children didn't know any better.
They didn't know that taking the tongues of our children would also protect our ways from them.
Now, the shame they taught is dying.
Our knowledge will be safe with our children now.
It is time to give them back their tongues.

Baba looked down at his fingers, rubbing something off his index finger with his thumb, as he sat looking at the freeze frame of me, with me. He looked at me, with a faint smile; its true depth hidden in the bigger sparkle of his eyes.

Our children's minds, bodies, and souls were enslaved by the machine.
In their greed, need for control, love of power, and cruelty, they forgot to steal our children's hearts.
Our children love us. They're looking for us. They want to come home.

It is time to help them come home. Bring the children home, nosisim.

I felt the pulse of the universe again, the heartbeat... (koosh koosh koosh). Knowing I would be leaving my grandfather yet again… and my grandmother, mother and aunts, who were talking and laughing in the kitchen behind me, not knowing the older me had come to visit. Leaving them with the 6 year old me who hadn't yet known the incredible loss of the kokum and mooshoom she sat there taking for granted would be here forever, I stifled a sob deep in my chest.

The murmur of the scene in the freeze-frame not so muted anymore; I looked at my grandfather and said, "My grandchildren are my secret weapon, Baba".

The Time Is Here.
KOOSH KOOSH KOOSH KOOSH
Then I fell out of the sky.

Who Are You ~~Without Colonialism?~~

Jihan Thomas

Who Are You ~~Without Colonialism~~?

~~without colonialism~~ I am
~~without colonialism~~ I feel the heat
~~without colonialism~~ I hear the messages
~~without colonialism~~ I already knew the colors
~~without colonialism~~ I know the codes
~~without colonialism~~ I been giving life
~~without colonialism~~ I been had the seeds
~~without colonialism~~ I have love
~~without colonialism~~ I don't need no words
~~without colonialism~~ I been the universe
~~without colonialism~~ I feed the planet
~~without colonialism~~ I know whose child I am
~~without colonialism~~ I know who I guard
without colonialism IAMNOTYOURS

34 • JIHAN THOMAS

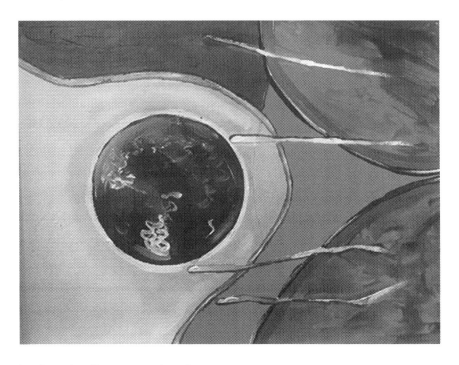

Medium: Acrylic on canvas board
Size: 8x11
Date: 2022

Within the Me

Anthony C. Guerra

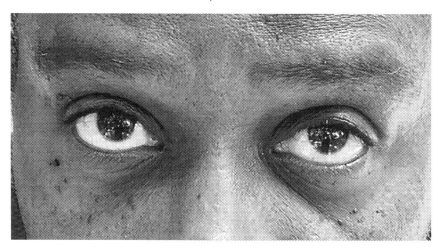

> When we revolt,
> is not for a particular culture.
> We revolt simply because, for many reasons,
> we cannot breathe.
> — *Franz Fanon*

Me without colonialism is the purpose-self, the nature-self with the energy and spirituality of that Oneness.

Within the Me (2023). To access Within the me, click on the image above or copy and paste the following link: https://vimeo.com/user204975447/withintheme?share=copy

Coming with the ability to experience and express one's cultural foundations is fundamental to one's growth and development. My understanding of culture, rooted in my Afro Caribbean '**Blackground'** and the Knowledge shared by my elders and ancestors, is all these things: NAME, LANGUAGE, LAND, HOUSING, CLOTHING, FOOD, DANCE, MUSIC, ART, SCIENCE, LITERATURE, THEATRE… Culture is then divided into Feelings, Beliefs and Emotions which guide my relations and shape my traditions and ceremonies, aiding navigation in the world. The word dance indicates energy in a state of quality, that's what the word 'da' means, life force or energy, knowing oneself.

This offering honors the four elements, harmonizing with the energies associated with Fire, Water, Air and Earth. My culture codes this understanding in our ceremonies, dances and day-to-day behaviour. The dance starts from the center and it spirals to its power points. Using traditional steps, I express Fire through vibrations and the flicking of the feet, Water with the undulation of the body and limbs, Air with the twirling of the arms and spinning action, and Earth with the pounding of the feet and the trashing of the arms or pulling apart.

Without colonialism, I am. I am not a position or space. I do not hold status in delusional state. I do not wear a suit of armour. I cannot be confined. I am light.

As an Afro -Caribbean man, I am shaped by bloods and cultures from many continents. I am the colonized and the colonizer. Being decolonized in dance means being be able to recognize, identify, separate and reconstruct all the aspects of self that are layered within my culture.

When I dance, I sing, I work, I play and I pray. That is me without colonization or the shadow. My dance expresses an acknowledgement: All aspects of me, the elements, the energies, and spirit as I …breath…!

Octavio Quintanilla. A Micro-Essay on the "Micro-Essays on Poetics."

Micro-Essay on Poetics #7." 10"x10" Mixed media on linen finish paper.

Time Immemorial

Amanda Buffalo

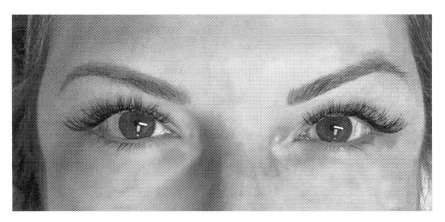

My bellybutton connects me to
constellations of Ancestral love
fractals of stardust in TimeSpace
woven through connections that multiply
into a confluence of interests

presencing and represencing
through the generations
a messy serendipity
of quantum entanglement
lovingly crafted by a grandmother's hands
in familiar worlds unknown

a dew drop in a web
of cycle-reciprocal networks
that move at the speed of light
infinite in the forms I can take
reduced to be human
this time around
though galaxies live
inside me

I am where the world ends
and also, where it begins
again
young as I will ever be
old as the universe itself
my body a black hole
where galaxies come to rest, replenish, and transform
ambling towards the light
to be born and reborn
a recycled dinosaur
from days past

I come from a minute or millennia of matriarchies
that birthed me into being
from prayer
beyond the binaries of
Creator and Creation
breathed into life
awakened by suffering
and exhaled into
the gift of death
a thousand times
in cycles of transmutation
and regeneration

the universe exists in me,
and as me
the land is the same -
it is in me and as me
through generations
and generations
and generations

like the migratory patterns
of the caribou
my body is a sacred
conversation with the land
whispered on blades of long grass
rippled to the water's edge

I am matter
in the process of mattering
and when all that remains
are my remains in the ground
a ceremony of sacred belonging
returns me home
to what I have always been

the land
nothing
but the land

welcome home,
Grandchild.

Octavio Quintanilla. A Micro-Essay on the "Micro-Essays on Poetics."

Micro-Essay on Poetics #8." 10"x10" Mixed media on linen finish paper.

liberation

c.k. samuels

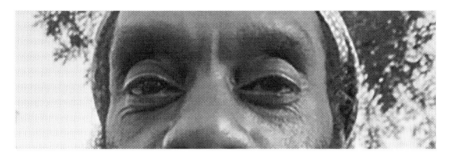

This land allows me myself. This land is my caretaker. This land has given me knowledge before any human or human creation. Standing in a field, I see images of people—singly and in groups—crossing this land with offerings to give and offerings received. Now I benefit from the knowledge kept with the Haudenosaunee, Kanien'Kehá:ka, Wendake-Nionwentsio and Anishnabewaki Nations. With Knowledge comes duty. I hope my performance of this duty is pleasing to the ancestral energy coursing through my body and this land.

liberation

I went to ask a teacher
if it was possible
for a world to exist
for me to be me
and not someone else

but I knew the answer
so I really went to ask the teacher
what it is we should do
for us to be as we are
and to love the beauty of our creator

I thought I needed
liberation from
being unsettled
while seeking impossibilities
of perfection

I learned that
unsettled is fluid
rootless, nomadic, and transient
- implying freedom
a freedom to
embrace imperfection
and be closer to wild
I learned that
unsettled is worried and uneasy
- implying empathy
and capacity to share experience
unsettled
is closer to wild
so now I think I need
liberation to
be unsettled
to be open to experience
to be free to feel

I went to ask a teacher
if it was possible
for a world to exist
where there was just need to do
and just done

I needed to know
where we should go
to escape the self-affirmation
of 'hate and destroy' nations
while living in jungles of concrete and vegetation
where paths are many
strewn with peril
leading to sanctuary

on journeys of escape
with maps to be read

and signs to be seen
we need
liberation to
be unsettled
to be open to experience
to be free to feel

in jumbles of information confusion
- each medium seeking control
of the human's command of behaviour
sowing seeds to doubt
that ants, grass, butterflies
and those birds
those seasonal journeyers
through this land of four nations
offer glorious sights into instinctual lives
of all our relations -
we need
liberation to
be unsettled
to be open to experience
to be free to feel
to be closer to wild

to receive guidance on ways to more liberation
the teacher nodded
the teacher rose
the teacher said:

liberation

what you think gets you places
what you want gets you places
what you need gets you places
so what do you think about liberation

do you think it is possible
to power your way through life
to be in control of yourself

do you think about
liberation from
thoughts of property and its use
liberation from ownership and rent
liberation to relate with land
to relate with vitality
to repair division in our social fabric
liberating worth from abode

and mode of living

do you want to be free
to do what you love
do you want us to see
who you could really be

do you want to have
liberation from
currency
freedom to flow
to give gifts presence
to make them current
becoming currency
entering general usage
as bottomless sources of harmonic production

it could be liberation is what you need
it could be liberation is your steed
as you take life for a ride

you might need
liberation from
exile
freedom to
relate with ancestors
of today and tomorrow

to hear their voice
to follow their call
to see their paths
to feel their ways

ways to more liberation

liberation of saharan dust
knowing unity of all land
where every destruction is creation
where god and the devil
are together in the same house
if they are two

liberation from
adjectives
and the imposition of value
where
you can walk on both sides
of a line
and it is still just as balanced

as deep voyages
above and below
which create the friction-based balance
of doing time on both sides

a balance that finds peace
in war

i was quiet
the teacher continued:

do your things
and do them with pleasure

you can choose what you think
and what you think
gets you places

i was quiet
this time the teacher joined me
so i waited a while
then i rose
unsettled
one of many
carried in currents of air and water
living members in surroundings
each on our own path
each in our own way
together

48 • c.k. samuels

Octavio Quintanilla. A Micro-Essay on the "Micro-Essays on Poetics."

Micro-Essay on Poetics #9." 10"x10" Mixed media on linen finish paper.

A Love Letter to Myself

Jackie Lee

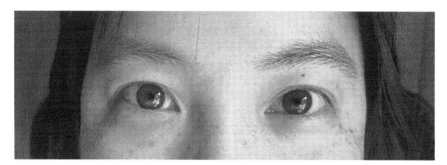

Dear restlessness,

Who am I without colonialism? This is a love letter to myself, not anyone else. To acknowledge my inner voice, the conflicted aching, and all the unanswered quests that my ancestors and elders left behind.

Perhaps without colonialism, I will not be as bitter as I am this year. All that anger in my chest, in my veins, pounds at the sight and thought of it. The world has taught me how to steal and be greedy. This institution has taught me how to cheat, steal, and lie; I have learned to be entitled to what I think is mine and **demand** for it. My ancestors, my elders, and my history watch me bleed to death from fighting, stabbing, and screaming to protect what I claim to be mine. Recently, the summer wind whispered softly in my ears … *whatever I think is mine was never mine to begin with*. This land does not belong to me, to anyone. I stand still and listen, watching the willow leaves dance as the wind blows, wondering, where if not here do I belong?

…

    Ng, 伍, my grandmother from my father's side. When she stood on top of the mountain
after spending nights and days bribing, begging, swimming, and smuggling through the borders with 5 kids and 1 in the belly, I wondered if she stood still for a minute to listen to the wind and ask the moon where she belongs. I wondered if she looked back at the war as she took her first step into the new world that was also stolen through wars and bloodsheds? As she walked forward, she walked towards a new freedom that was promised to her by a crown. She traded in her family, heritage, connections, and roots, and exchanged them for *freedom*. While the wind whispers into her ears, only she would be able to say if it is worth it after all.

…

    Wu, 胡, my grandmother from my mother's side. As tourists rushed through the doors to see the Golden Gate, she stepped into the airport being and feeling brave, hurt, angry, confused, anxious, and hatred, while holding two children in her hands. Did she look back? Was there a second of hesitation of what she was about to embark on? If I am the dove that was resting on the light post as I watch my beloved Wu walking into the airport, I can imagine her heavy, bleeding, agonizing heart. She gave her hopes and dreams to the person she said—I do—and to a far away new country that promises dreams, but all she has now is a patriarchal ending. If she rolls her sleeves up, I might see bruises. The tear that hangs on her lower eyelids, tears of bravery, because she knows this land does not belong to her and she does not want it either. She knows she is going home.

…

    So where do I belong? I ponder this as I sat among my cousins at our family's 52th anniversary dinner celebrating how Ng brought us all to the new worlds and left Communism behind. I looked over at Ng's table, she was sitting among her siblings and children. To her left are the two siblings that she took with her as they crawled their way over the borders 52 years ago. To her right are the two other siblings that she left behind in the old world. They eventually made their way out independently without Ng.
    I see them all laughing and smiling, cheering with drinks and catching up politely, as if Ng's family was not broken, abandoned, politically and physically separated 52 years ago. At this moment, tears and betrayal were erased. I looked at my cousins, half of us grew up with *freedom* Ng consequently brought for us, the other half grew up without *freedom* because Ng wouldn't take their mothers and fathers with her 52 years ago. And 52 years later, we all gathered here on this land… well, another stolen land, awkward and embarrassed. Why aren't we

asking, "why are we here?" Why aren't we asking why some were not chosen 52 years ago? Why aren't they asking…. asking… "Why this land?"

As I packed my belongings into my bags, I travel from one land to the next, searching for answers, searching for a home. Searching for a land, a home, that is innocent, that is pure, that is blameless, where my soul can finally rest without guilt. And this is why I will never be able to stop travelling, moving, and searching. A land without guilt does not exist simply because all lands were once stolen by greedy thieves. We are thieves. I am a thief. Until we/I realize that, we/I will never find peace.

As I stood and watched the willow tree dance, I placed my bags down beside me, and reached my hand out into the wind and held hands with my past, my history, my ancestors, and my elders. I told them that I will be okay with this new peace I found in my heart, and that I can hear the music birds singing on the willow tree.

The one that stopped travelling,
李詠彤

Shauna Landsberg

Shauna Landsberg

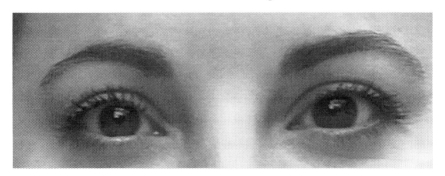

My name is Shauna Landsberg <Shoshanna Bat Reuben Pesach>, an Ashkenazi Jewish woman. This is a story of learning alongside my ancestors and the journey to understand it with Wisdom in the pursuit of Tikkun Olam <repairing the world> and Tzedek <justice>.

In this remembering of my history, I share the internal regenerations and rereadings of lessons from Jewish written and oral Torah, mystical interpretations, historical Hebrew and other language Jewish texts, and teachers both named and yet to be identified. I have intentionally omitted any publication credits for the texts and sites developed over centuries that cannot be owned. In honor of traditional oral practice, I try to name all speakers in the text by name and where they call home whenever possible. All publication years of references align with the Jewish calendar year. When specific publication dates were not available, the date of January 1 of the given year was used for calculating the Jewish year of publication. According to my ancestors' patronymic tradition, names appear as first and then last names in citations. Hebrew names were not used by many of my ancestors. Naming them all in this form is a piece of the re-connecting on my path. Translations between English and Hebrew appear in carats. My dream: To remember and relearn more Hebrew and Yiddish words and their origins.

I am divine plurality of singularity. In Judaism, the word Ain Sof is Infinite Being, absolute unity; zero. We learn from written words of the Jewish mystics in texts, like the *Sefer Yetzirah* (Ancestors, 3800), *Bahir* (Ancestors, 3860), and *Zohar* (Ancestors, 4960), that there are thirty-two paths to wisdom <chakhmah>, introduced in Hebrew liturgy through the thirty-two times that God's name of Elohim appears in the first chapter of Genesis describing the thirty-two facets of creation. The ten digits <sephar> and twenty-two letters that create text <sepher> of the Hebrew alphabet <aleph-bet> together represent these faces. The digits quantify, and the letters qualify. We transform these into communication through the third dimension by combining the two into written and spoken words. Unsurprisingly, in English, the word cypher derives from the Hebrew word sephar. They are connected. They talk to each other. The ten digits are the ten Sefirot, the basic concepts of existence. The twenty-two letters are categorized between the three Mothers, the twelve Elementals, and the seven Doubles. The work lev <heart> represents the paths <nativ> of Understanding <binah>. Wisdom is the father <abba>, and Understanding is the mother <immah>. Aryeh Kaplan's commentary on the Sefer Yetzirah (5750) reminds us that Wisdom is the water contained within and flowing through the river's path. It is also said that Wisdom is within the mind where understanding is verbalized. So, I must write and speak my understanding here (Aryeh Kaplan, 5750).

My soul came from above, from the stars where my ancestors reside. It was the spark that catalyzed my father's life force and my mother's egg. I was born in Shevat in the 11th month of the year. It is one beyond ten, eleven, the holy of holies. The letter for this month is tzadi. The word tzaddiq means righteous or just person. The words of Rabbi Aaron L. Raskin, when discussing the astrological significance of the month of Shevat, remind me: After the ten, when we turn to eleven. We make a "quantum leap" by turning to and surrendering to the Other (and the other) for Wisdom. This is a time when we turn "negative to positive." The letters in the word form an acronym meaning "the month of good news." It is a time for breaking with the old boundaries, systems, and ideas to bring forth fresh knowledge for the future (R. Aaron L. Raskin, 5778).

The astrological sign of Shevat is the water bearer, the constellation D'li, known in Western astrology as Aquarius. D'li more accurately translates to a pail or bucket. When I say the word D'li, I feel the tone and vibration of a drop of water hitting deep the surface of a well or a gulping sound that quenches thirst. We use D'li to carry water from one place to another. D'li collects knowledge from one place and carries it to another. Many examples in the *Torah* of Tzaddiqim (righteous people) and the month of Shevat include bringing the Jewish people

Shauna Landsberg • 55

Jewish ancestors created this mosaic pavement of a 42nd-century synagogue at Beth Alpha, Emek Yizri'el <Jezreel Valley>, Northern Palestine (4200).

from turmoil to harmony and preparing gifts for the next generation. With positive comes negative, and for all the humanitarian bravery, idealism, and pursuit of knowledge, the air sign can turn inward, into the mind, into oneself, into darkness. The bucket cannot hold water when it is full of silt and clay (Shaul Youdkevitch, 5779).

My ancestors preserved and protected this knowledge through their work, love, dreams, and within their own bodies and DNA. The thirty-two aspects of creation, the thirty-two mystical or hidden <peliyot> paths are imprinted on different parts of the human body: limbs, organs, and nervous system. They describe the cardinal direction, map the planets and orbits, the elements, light, darkness, atoms, flowers, animals, clay, seasons, months, and years—reflected in our bodies.

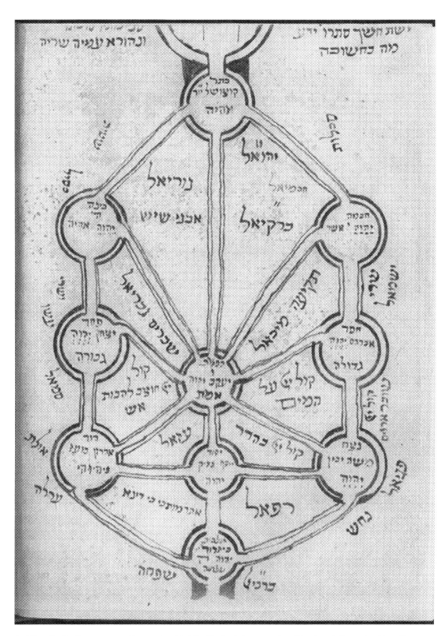

A Classic Sefirot tree—From the Kabbalistic Manuscript Sha'arei Ora shel by R. Yosef Gikatilla circa 5008 (5754).

Shauna Landsberg • 57

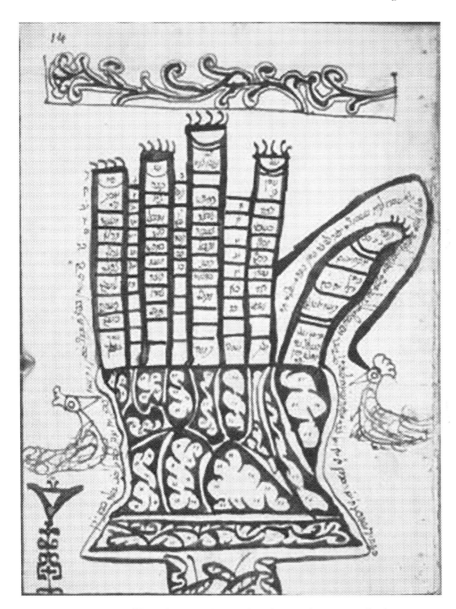

Hand Diagram in Josef ben Shem Tov ben Yeshu'ah 'ai's She'erit Yosef, Algeria circa 5564 (S. T. ben Y. De Faro, 5758).

58 • SHAUNA LANDSBERG

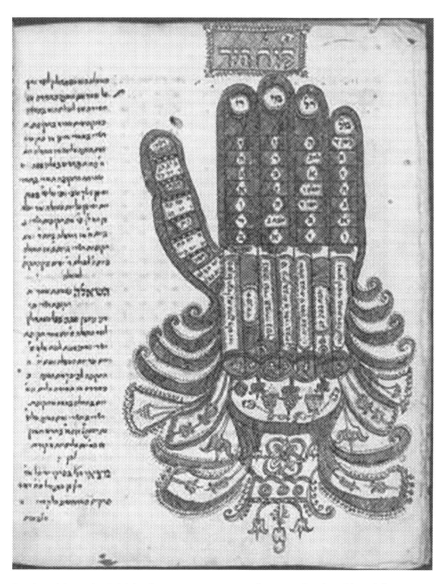

Retrieved from the British Library Manuscript Archives. Calendrical hand diagram Molad Yitsḥak in Sefer Evronot by Isaac Katzenellenbogen. Poland (5450).

A reminder that all that exists is a piece of the puzzle, coded with the same pattern, expressed in all the facets of the infinite. All Seferot <texts/books> to read. Each day I rediscover something in these thirty-two texts through the shape of their lines and the permutations of their letter, where they sit on my lips, tongue, and throat. I search for their equal in the rose and the snowflake.

I see my connection to the universe when I look at my hand. I have always been good with my hands, even though my left dominant hand holds "congenital defects," which worsen over time. A genetic mutation caused me to be born with an extra left thumb. They said it was useless and severed (it was not moved) when I was around 3 to 6 months old. My parents told me stories of how the plaster cast was almost the same size as me, and I would still try to hold things with it and suck on my missing thumb. (The Sefer Yetzirah shows the left thumb as binah <understanding>. Did I have an extra binah? Was it taken? How does this change shapes my path?) The parts comprising my left thumb that remain are misshapen; my nerves are missing in some places, they appear in places they shouldn't, and spiral into a dense, sensitive, seed-like neuroma at the base of my thumb in the bottom-left quadrant of my palm.

When I was a child, the neuroma was much larger than it is now, like the size of a quail egg. It wrapped around and encased a tendon or ligament, and they feared the growing tumor, although benign, would cause loss of mobility as I aged. My tiny hands became strong and skilled using the hammer and jigsaw as tools for creativity and reinvention, building toys and shelters out of the discarded scraps I found in my new development neighborhood in Kentucky.

I grew up with my mom mostly, and every new house we moved into was a two-person fix-up job. I painted, screwed, dug, peeled, and imagined the possibility of renewal out of the old. My mother was a nurse, and my father is a surgeon. No one would describe my father as patient, but this virtue shines through when approaching a lesson with the triangulated skills of body coordination, tools, and planning. Whether learning new sports, handicrafts, simple medical procedures, kneading hamburger meat with the perfect concoction of additional ingredients or driving a car. Although my father and I may have fewer commonalities than my four other siblings, we share a special connection because I was always open and eager to learn from him in these ways. Neither my parents saw my my left hand as a hindrance. They treated it as a new way of knowing and being, embracing my ability to perform tasks with both hands, even as they stumbled in figuring out how to instruct my body in mirrored relation to theirs. I learned how to use a hooked needle and tweezers to tie stitches into my stuffed animals and do it backwards with my dominant left hand. I wove intricate bracelets and became proficient in untangling complicated knots. Even though my left hand moved slightly differently, I loved playing the piano and feeling the vibration through my fingers. In middle school and through surgeries, I found ways to play my oboe in band class while healing. I switched to the percussion section when I had only one functioning hand—the hands.

Once the doctors believed I had almost stopped growing around age twelve, they tried to remove it. At each severed end, they attached a salvaged blood vessel, hypothesizing that my youth and the path laid by the blood vessel would allow the connective tissue to regrow. My arm was wrapped in large dressings, like a boxing glove, for a couple of months. I had to rely on my right hand and find strength and dexterity in this mirror companion. Although my left hand continues to change, causing me some trouble over time, it serves me daily. Its frayed nerves manage to write, type, grasp, squeeze, carry, open, close, hold, mend, tie, build, caress, and knit (a lot of knitting). Knitting and building are activities that bring me closest to my ancestors. Because of them, I have the wisdom and understanding to envision and move deeper into the unknown with bravery. When I bring my hands together to recreate, not only do I grow closer to my familial ancestors, I grow closer to those "beyond the binary" as their gifts slide through my fingers (Clelia O. Rodríguez, 5782). My saliva mixes with the fibers of the wool; I wrap the yarn around the bamboo and steel; I slide the stitches along the circular path as they catch loose strands of my long, dark, brown hair in their grasp; I feel the physics of these elements in my tension, the body and earth combined. I see the spiral pattern reflected in the pale green monstera leaf as it yearns to unfurl. I remember my ancestors' connection to the land within our body and the knowledge still carried in our language, stories, holidays, and tears.

As I grow my relationships with my ancestors, so grows my yearning to learn more Yiddish and Hebrew language, and read the music, stories, art, and all the ways they communicate across all continents from generation to generation < l'dor v'dor>. The search often leads to seemingly dead ends, especially in the stories of our mothers, grandmothers, and foremothers beyond the binary, a political teaching and radical learning framework I learned from Clelia O. Rodríguez. *I remind myself these paths are not meant to be easy. These threads are hidden in their very nature for protection.* If there is one thing all Jews can agree on regarding of our ethnicity, spirituality, and organized religion, it is that Jews *are required* to **question**. Criticality is key. To wrestle with texts over dinner tables and street carts, in shuls (the Yiddish term for synagogue) and gardens, or through correspondence and manuscripts written over centuries. We are ***especially*** required to question everything re: G-O-D and all its in-betweens. We are all part of the same story—past-present-future—in one, and each being breathes new life into the text for the coming generation.

In the often hidden stories of our female ancestors emerge 13 archetypes of the Divine Feminine, as shared by Jill Hammer and Taya Shere in *The Hebrew Priestess* (5775):

1. Weaver <Oreget>
2. Prophetess <Neviah>
3. Shrinekeeper <Tzovah>
4. Witch< Ba'alat Ov>

5. Maiden < Na'arah>
6. Mother <Eim>
7. Queen <Gevirah>
8. Midwife <Meyaledet>
9. Wise Woman <Chachamah>
10. Mourning Woman <Mekonenet>
11. Seeker <Doreshet>
12. Lover <Ohevet> and
13. Fool <Leitzanit>.

They also represent the holy, mystical, and priestly duties bestowed upon them. I experience them each as gates/gaits to the paths. My ancestors light my way. As I remember their stories, I feel how they embodied priestly roles through their paths in life.

I am walking the path of the Oreget <Weaver Priestess>, showing reverence for the web of life and grounding me to earth like the roots of the Tree of Life <Etz Chaim.>. On this path, my task is to see the truth and beauty in every thread, recognizing each of the fibers that coil and twist into one, twisting like the umbilical cord that roots me to my mother. Although these threads may be thin or frayed, I, as weaver, re-define intentionally to entwine with my hands patterns of numbers, shapes, and loops into one rich tapestry. I look at my palm and see the nerves winding into my palm, into the soil. How does my weaving connect me to the earth and my motherly path?

Judaism is full of symbolic objects, traditionally created, maintained, and protected by women. Ancient Israelites and Canaanites worshipped the weaver goddess Asherah, the priestesses adorning and guarding her. As Asherah, mother to all, weaves life, the Oreget reveres this creative force in the world around her (Jill Hammer, 5775). When we know the pattern in our bodies, we can weave garments and canopies to honor mother earth and our divine connection. We "dress" the Torah scrolls in adorned vestments before returning them home in the arc. Prayer shawls, or tallis in Yiddish, four connect our bodies to the corners of the earth, adorned with knotted and coiled tzitzit (a feminine word in Hebrew) <tassles> at each corner. Each twist and fastening is intentional. We also use the tallis to create the chuppah <canopy> for weddings.

*****

My second great-grandfather, Jacob Glassman, Aaron Zelig ben Moshe, was a contractor from a shtetl outside of current day Minsk, Belarus. He was from the tribe of Levi, a Levite. Levites carry the tribal responsibility of serving the priests, a primary duty being constructing the houses of worship. I am not one to dwell over the literality of the tribes of Jacob, yet it seems like a fitting association in my grandfather Jacob's case. After fleeing from his home Eastern Europe and arriving in Toronto (via a few years stopover in London, England), he continued his trade by building some of the oldest synagogues in Toronto, the first being Anshei Minsk, located in the neighborhood of Kensington Market. I try to stop by the shul, or "The Minsker" as they called it, anytime I find myself near the neighborhood. Less than a hundred years ago, there were more than thirty synagogues in and around Kensington Market; there are two remaining today: The Kiever and The Minkser (*Anshei Minsk Synagogue | The Downtown Toronto Shul*, n.d.; *The Kiever Shul*, n.d.).

I find myself walking through Kensington and realize it has been over a year since I visited her, Anshei Minsk, here on St. Andrew Street. I have never been inside. As I pause now, I don't recall ever touching the building or its steps.

I picked up a small rock of old concrete as I walked down Spadina. I couldn't find a stone or rock. I approached the steps, and the neighbors enjoying a relaxing afternoon on her wide staircase, slowly departed. Perhaps they felt this conversation required privacy. I touched the wall, the bricks, and the weathered wood of the doors. I chanted the Mourner's Kaddish aloud as my toes touched the doorstep. I set the asphalt scrap in my palm in the corner at the top of the stairs. I stepped away and gazed upon her lines and shapes.

I put my backpack on the ground, sat down on the front entrance steps and took out the Sefer Yetzirah to read. Above me: Thirty-two paths appear inscribed on the façade of the building in the sequence 32–10–3–12–7. I watched people walking by. I observed pedestrians gazing up. Twenty minutes passed. I heard people whispering in various languages as they passed by. I wonder: Do they question who she was and where she came from. I continue to sit there. I noticed cigarette butts, litter and weeds growing tall within the cracks in the sidewalks. I contemplated the shul. It seemed like a miracle she is still standing there, facing the sun, wrinkled with the passing of time. I noticed the names inscribed on the walls facing the street. Who sits within her womb each day to pray? Who mends her so she can provide shelter? Who adorns her appendages with metal and fiber? Who speaks her name? I want people to know her name Anshei Minsk, The Minsker.

As I continue to sit, I pause and remember. I feel it in my gut. I feel back further into the past, past the place, and to the land <ha'aretz>, to The Earth Mother <Shekhina>. Before my great-grandparents bought pieces of her skin as parceled land from British and Irish settlers; sold to them by the British estate holder George Taylor Denison; sold to him by British colonial administrators in strips named Park Lots 16, 17, and 18 (Bruce Beaton, 5777). Before the British, French, and Dutch colonizers pillaged and stole the land through oppressive force and bad-faith treaties, choosing to ignore the threads that to connect back to their ancestral respect for land and their duty Indigenous peoples on this part of Turtle Island. The land they call this land T'karonto, now translated to "The Meeting Place" in the Mohawk language (Denise Bolduc et al., 5781, p. 21). A time before her body was objectified and defiled and her parts were named by those who took ownership of her through force. Artist Ange Loft <Kanien'kehá:ka>, from Kahnawà:ke,

Quebec, Canada remembers, through the teachings of her community and ancestors that "[T'karonto] was a seasonal meeting place, a place for trade and ongoing council. It's a place where Indigenous Nations have come together to remember and relate going back thousands of years" (Ange Loft, n.d.; Denise Bolduc et al., 5781, p. 17)." A place for connection, consensus, and collective remembering of the past and future, a place where her paths weave together and waters combine for the sake of current and future generations. I am connected to and stand upon stolen Indigenous land. I cannot walk humbly upon a just path, I cannot weave as Oreget, I cannot carry as D'li, or know love, wisdom, understanding, or motherhood unless I learn from the Indigenous people here today who know their place here and their relationship to Shekhina and the facet of her face in T'karonto. I have a responsibility to count her rivers and learn their names, to understand where on her body she shares materials to sustain and shelter our bodies like her own, to know how each of these nations adorned and protected her so she could bear this fruit in reciprocity. My counting has barely begun, and it's not okay.

I fished a loonie out of my pocket and walked around the corner to a Canada-themed tourist shop. "May I please buy two plastic bags? That's all." The cashier replies, "Ten cents each. How many do you want?" I pause. My rationale for two was that one would serve as a glove as I picked up the litter, and the other would be my trash bag. I answer the cashier, "I think three should be good."

I walked back to the shul where I began picking up the trash. I felt like a bird preening her feathers as I gather the tangles of weeds and trash. I soon unburdened myself of my backpack, placed it on the lowest step, and returned to collecting. I saw a man sitting halfway up the steps in the sun. He asked, "Do you have another bag so I can help?" I waved hello and said, "Thanks so much. No, no, no, please relax; enjoy your smoke now." I felt a warmth in my chest and body, seeing him sitting still on her steps. I was honored to see someone appreciate her. He insisted, "No, no. Please let me help. I come to sit here all the time. I want to help. Do you have another bag?" I went to my backpack and pulled out the third bag.

We continued to chat as we cleaned. He tells me he lives in the shelter across the street. "I arrived here from my country three weeks ago. I like to come to sit here in the sun. There are few places just to go sit around here. What is this place? To me, it looks like a court or government or something." I explained that I like to stop by when I'm in the neighborhood and see my ancestor's work, and I want to show appreciation for the building and everyone who has helped keeping her there. I asked him if he had any family or friends here from his country to which he responded with a "Not yet." We took turns yanking on the sturdier weeds, looping back over the same path, picking up remnants overlooked. He told me a bit about his job back home as a professional truck driver and how not being employed in Canada made him feel like he had no use in Canada—sitting and waiting most of the days, waiting for paperwork

We filled the bags to the brim and tied them. I took his bag and mine in hand. We exchanged a handshake, our fingernails and skin embedded with dirt and chlo-

Close-up of the front exterior of Anshei Minsk Synagogue on St. Andrew Street built and maintained by the congregants and the Kensington Market community.

rophyll. I told him that my ancestors would be very happy of this connection. I turned back to admire her face again and said goodbye until I am in the area again. She looked renewed. I began counting the lines and shapes. I saw the fingers of her hand above the two doors. At the top of the stone moulding, I noticed the scalloped cups that run along the length. Thirty-two.

REFERENCES

Ancestors. (ca. 4200). *Beth Alpha* [Mosaic]. https://commons.wikimedia.org/wiki/File:Beit_Alpha.jpg

Anshei Minsk Synangogue. (n.d.). *Anshei Minsk synagogue: The downtown Toronto shul.* (n.d.). Retrieved 30 Av 5783, from https://www.theminsk.com/

Beaton, B. (5777, Av). *Kensington Market.* The Canadian Encyclopedia. https://www.the-canadianencyclopedia.ca/en/article/kensington-market

Bolduc, D., Gordon-Corbiere, M., Tabobondung, R., & Wright-McLeod, B. (5781). *Indigenous Toronto: Stories that carry this place.* Coach House Books.

Chan, A. (5757). *The spirit of the dragon: The story of Jean Lumb, a proud chinese-canadian.* Dundurn Press.

Gikatilla, J. b. A. (5758). *Gates of light: = Sha'are orah* (Avi Weinstein, Ed. & Trans.). Altamira Press.

Hammer, J. (5775). *The Hebrew priestess: Ancient and new visions of Jewish women's spiritual leadership.* Ben Yehuda Press.

Kaplan, A. (5750). *Sefer Yetzirah: The book of creation.* S. Weiser.

Katzenellenbogen, I. (ca. 5450). *(Molad Yitsḥaḳ) Sefer Evronot* (or_9782_f014r). British Library. https://www.bl.uk/manuscripts/Viewer.aspx?ref=or_9782_f014r

The Kiever Shul. (n.d.). *The historic kiever synagogue: A jewel in the heart of downtown Toronto.* Retrieved 30 Av 5783. https://www.kievershul.com

Loft, A. (n.d.). *Ange Loft: About.* Retrieved 30 Av 5783, from https://www.angeloft.ca/about

Raskin, R. A. L. (5778). *The zodiac of shevat—The Kabbalah of the Jewish months.* Chabad-Lubavitch Media Center. https://www.chabad.org/multimedia/video_cdo/aid/3840329/jewish/The-Zodiac-of-Shevat.htm

Rodríguez, C. O. (5782, Shevat). *Transnational pedagogies of liberation.* https://www.youtube.com/watch?v=rILLLL8dBPc

Shem Tov ben Yakob De Faro (ca. 5758). *Sefer ha-yiḥud* (Mahadurah biḳortit ha-mevuseset ʻal 29 kive yad, kolel mavo, ḥilufe nusḥaʼot u-marʼe meḳomot ʻal yede Refaʼel Kohen.). R. Kohen.

Youdkevitch, S. (5779). *Shevat—Aquarius.* Live Kabbalah. https://livekabbalah.org/shevat-aquarius/

unscripted

Künsang

Editorial Note: This chapter has been edited and adapted from a private email exchange, that followed a book meeting where the pedagogical political framework of the question *who are you without colonialism* was presented following Indigenous ways of knowing that fall under what is "understood" by some in academia as decolonizing. Künsang was given colour, to contextualize the question, in addition to other anchoring ideas, invitations, and political pedagogical calls from Clelia O. Rodríguez and her Ancestors.

*****

Three moonrises and sunrises.
Visual journaling of interbeing.
Tonight's moonlight is to offer my intention.
I know only today. My mind tomorrow will not be the same as the mind of today and yesterday.

Knowing/nutrienting/microbing the soil for new seeds to be planted that are being harvested.

Harvesting, sharing the harvest, and knowing/nutrienting/microbing the soil before I can care for and bring seeds to be offered. Maybe planting the seed is after the October 2023 cycle.

Like butter rising to the top when the milk is churned, I cannot know what may rise when harvesting, sharing the harvest, and knowing/nutrienting/microbing the soil before harvesting new seeds to plant and share. I was born in the Water year . . . harvesting this season in the Black Water Tiger Year has been [no English word to express]. How I am harvesting this season in the Black Water Tiger cycle manifests the nutrienting/microbing of the soil for the new seeds to be planted.

I offer my intention and how I am sensing.

Smoothie of feelings in the Black Water Tiger Year (2022).

*****

I do not know what my color would be without colonialism.

"My color" connects with spirit.

I felt an invisible undercurrent of darkness that I could not see and touch as a kid.

What is the color for something I sense, yet cannot see, touch, and grasp in my hands as a kid when no one teaches and shows me?

I began to see, touch, and grasp the invisible undercurrent . . . and name them much later as an adult. Colonialism normalizes to the point of not being easily identifiable. At one time in my life, I did not know that my attitudes, views, words, and more linked with colonialism. Searching to understand myself, and the invisible undercurrents, eventually I came to learn that silence is among the forms of survival and moving forward. I had to learn how the energy behind silence was being released, similar to the shoots of rhizomes growing laterally underground and then shooting upwards above the soil.

What color would I be without silence?

Then, I learned how the invisible undercurrents show up in my genes, DNA, nervous system, neurobiology, and psyche.

One story. When I started secondary school, it was my first time seeing Japanese American students. A salient feeling or instinct arose with discomfort in my body. This was one of the invisible undercurrents that I had sensed during my secondary school years. There were no causes and events that I had experienced to dislike Japanese people. Nothing to point to, such as media content. No memory to connect to before I started secondary school. Then, later during the school year, I learned that Japan had colonized Korea. I remember this reaction and inner dialogue: "Oh, yes! Of course, that is what happened. Everything makes sense now." And I felt a sense of closure. Then, I forgot about those days.

unscripted • 69

> I cannot recall if it was in high school, my 20s, or 30s . . . one day...
>
> I remembered those days and wondered...
> how it was possible for an inner intuition to arise,
> to stay distant and
> to feel that Japanese people were my enemies.

I had no previous encounters or knowledge. No internet back then. Maybe in a past life, I had lived at a time of war, military aggression, or colonial oppression at the hands of Japan's soldiers. Maybe the salient feeling came from these times. Maybe the salient feeling from that time in my youth was one of the many invisible undercurrents living in my nervous system and inherited through epigenetics that had resurfaced in explicit form.

> What color would I be without the imprints of invisible undercurrents that had passed from generation to generation?

It has taken my entire lifetime to search and name the invisible undercurrents I first sensed as a kid. I learned how my body, mind, and spirit became vessels of unresolved wounds and scars from generation to generation. The more I learned, the more I noticed these in their explicit to subtle forms within myself.

> What is the color of remembrance?
> What is the color of restoring and preserving culture?
> What is the color of language?
> What is the color of heritage and ancestry?

Buddhism is a deep part of my Asian ancestry and cultural identity.

> What color would I be with the undoing of whiteness in Buddhism in America?

> What color would I be without the racialization of Asian and Asian American Buddhists in the United States?

> What color would I be without the behaviors of religious appropriation and racial hegemony from the white Buddhist community?

The colonial oppression of Tibetans and systemic dismantling of their culture, language, and religion affect my spiritual life as well.

> What color would I be without the harms of colonialism in my birth country, culture, language, identity, and kinship to the communities in my Buddhist tradition?

I am conditioned to the point that what has not been normal is viewed and experienced as normal. With ongoing impact and the deep layers in the subconscious and gene expression levels, *how could I say and know, truthfully, what my color would be without colonialism?*

> What color would I be without colonialism?

Maybe if I could feel the messages of my body, I would sense the color of my being.

Who gets to gain knowledge and be the knowledge "expert" of what was passed onto my genes, DNA, spirit, and subconsciousness?

What becomes of my color with and without colonialism when, for the sake of "data," my story is aggregated and flattened to conveniently fit the biases and perceptions of a researcher, institution, activist, scholar, etc.?

I am the true knowledge holder of my story . . . and what my color would be without colonialism that has yet to come.

Color With Colonialism

Purple is the color I feel while living with colonialism.
Purple is the feeling of reciprocity in the human relationship.

"보라해 borahae (I purple you)."

"We purple you."

I say these sayings that come from BTS. Absorbing BTS messages into my life has been a journey and lifestyle of healing, inspiration, acceptance, and living fully. This year, 2023, is the anniversary of 10 years of BTS' messages being my lifelines when the soil of my spirit needed water and sunlight to go forward.

This is the feeling of purple for me.

I cannot grow in confinement. Messages, healing through music, inner transformations, and how I connect cannot be confined to one worldview. One approach. One path. One genre. The genre fluidity of BTS music, expression, style, and dance choreography has been a medium for helping me to expand how I sense and relate to my inner world meeting the outer world . . . and stretch and break the limitations of how I feel and view myself. The messages in BTS lyrics, videos, speeches, interviews, and more have been at the heart of my own cognitive reframing and the work of reparenting my own youth.

This is the feeling of purple for me.

보라해. I purple you. We purple you. Behind these words is social change. I create social change challenging racism, xenophobia, homophobia, discrimination, and cultural ignorance concerning BTS.

This is the feeling of purple for me.

I have wondered if the Korean language could have died if Japan's colonization had not ended. To lose language is to lose culture. I did not learn the Korean language because of socio-economic reasons and the stages of acculturation that had dominated my youth because of the perceived achievement mindset to build and "thrive" and not struggle to "survive." The last stage of acculturation is assimilation. I often connect cultural assimilation in the United States with the whitening and colonizing of my mind and speech. I reconnected with my Korean language because of BTS and A.R.M.Y.

This is how purple feels.

I can show, share, and teach Korean culture and stories to my nieces and nephew in a relevant way because of A.R.M.Y and BTS.

This is the joy of purple.

For the first time in my life, I was at a sold-out stadium with thousands of kids, youth, adults, and grandparents singing together the line "You've shown me I have reasons I should love myself." This was a feeling of "belonging": collective community and humanity. I get emotional knowing that fans learn Korean to sing along with the BTS lyrics, to understand their messages, and to learn the Korean culture. It was unimaginable, when I was a kid to even consider a stadium of people singing in Korean in the United States, Europe, and around the world. Rare. I always get goosebumps listening to fans in Brazil sing in Korean.

This is how purple feels.

The messages of BTS inspire me for Care, Community, and Nature.

This is how purple feels.

Purple has been the emotion, message, language, and code for trust, love, acceptance, and belonging.
Purple is not just a color. Purple is now a new word for a feeling I cannot find in English. I feel purple in my spirit, body, and mind.
Purple is the closest feeling to belonging for me with cultures, languages, and faith traditions.
When I visualize the undoing of colonization, the feeling of purple crosses frontiers, borders, and digital lines.
Purple is my revolutionary color in my daily life when I choose to speak and call in.

This is how purple feels.

What sound you would like to embody without colonialism and what sound you would be with it?

The sounds of the Buddhist mantras without and with colonialism; these would be my mantras for the liberation of the colonized body, speech, mind, and spirit.
Sanskrit mantra of Avalokiteśvara: oṃ maṇi padme hūṃ

Avalokiteśvara is the Bodhisattva of Compassion and embodies conventional and ultimate compassion. The ultimate compassion is beyond human conception.

A person can recite the mantra with the intention of working towards being the mind of Avalokiteśvara while living without and with colonialism.

A person can receive the proper lineage transmission and permission to practice as Avalokiteśvara and recite the mantra.

The mind of the Bodhisattva of Compassion is beyond the binary view.

Sanskrit mantra of the Heart Sūtra: gate pāragate pārasaṃgate bodhi svāhā

The Heart Sūtra (Sanskrit: Prajñāpāramitāhṛdaya, which translates as The Heart of the Perfection of Wisdom) contains the essence of the Buddha's teachings.

The mantra of the Heart Sūtra contains the Buddha's teachings from the beginning, middle, and end of the path of liberation. The teachings carry the stages and paths for liberation, the conventional Truth, and the ultimate Truth.

I imagine the wind carrying the mantras and the words and the intentions of the words and speakers being absorbed into the beings, land, and nature.

In what part of the Mother Earth do you feel more connected to the land (this could be also from the knowledge you may have heard from your Elders) and in what part of mother earth you are disconnected from?

I feel more connected with Trees regardless of their geo-location. Sometimes when I see a Tree, I sense the care and neglect of the land area. My senses call me to touch the Tree barks.

The sacred Bodhi Tree in Bodh Gaya, India, at the Mahabodhi Temple, is where I am most spiritually connected to. The Bodhi Tree at the Mahabodhi Temple is the only place in the world where I have the chance to walk and sit in the same shared space with Buddhists from many Asian cultures.

The part of Mother Earth I feel more disconnected from is the ocean. I understand water at the human scale. I have yet to know the depth of the ocean's power at the scale of nature beyond human conception, human intelligence, human ego, and human arrogance.

*****

Creation story on March 21, 2023

The creation story of a seed that is untitled because it was unscripted and unplanned. Throughout the day, I had been sensing something different inside me that I could not form into words myself. Words have limitations because these are the constructs created by people. Feelings have no limitations because the form and formlessness of the human body and mind are nature. And so, sometimes feelings have no words. Something was stirring within me and I had a feeling it had to do with synchronizing with nature. Then, I opened the computer desktop calculator. With no reason for doing so, I typed 0 divided by 0. Instead of 0 appearing, it showed as "result is undefined. Taken aback, these words were unexpected. It was my first time seeing this in a calculator. I had expected 0 as "the answer"—it was what I was trained to believe; it is the only logic of 0 x 0 and 0 ÷ 0 that I have known. Paused. Entered into contemplation, unintentionally. When I was contemplating on "result is undefined," I instinctively looked at the lunar calendar. No thought. No reason. Just an autoresponse. It said, "New Moon" day.

The sensibilities came together.

I recorded my contemplation in the living, present moment. The depth of what arose in my mind, heart, feelings, and body is in the moments of silence and pauses; and are not found in the recording. My reflection on "result is undefined" was on the Madhyamaka view of reality.

After the audio recording ended, I listened to my body and heart. That is how the creation story happened. The unplanned creation story itself was contemplative. The feeling in my heart and mind is the seed. My understanding is that no two moments are with the same karmic conditions.

Nature

My seed offering has been changing into an ode to nature as my first ancestor, first spiritual teacher, first wisdom teacher, and first compassion teacher.

What I wrote up to now is the understanding I have received from the interdependence with nature. Without colonialism and patriarchy, nature is my guide on being human.

I am creating with what comes and not through a predetermined goal or plan. The voice of the inner spirit is unplanned. Tomorrow is not here today. My mind five minutes ago is different from now.

My body senses may say today to draw images or change the verses to a story, haiku, or letter. I began creating in verses. Then, rewriting and rewriting. Maybe the rewriting is planting? Harvesting my mind? I wrote verses of three lines each. Body Speech Mind are three. Buddha Dharmā Saṃgha are three. Birth Life Death are three. Lines may change. Then, I noticed the verses were in the past tense. Past. How are the messages sustaining in the past tense? Seed is sustaining.

To make a handwritten seed instead of keyboarding the letters? The more I write, the more ideas come to my head. Rhizomes shoot upwards from the soil of my mind when I water my writing. The seed has its own pace and spirit . . . my body is its messenger. Though the seed is not ready, today, I offer my idea.

*****

When I offer water bowls on the altar, it is filled with deep meaning—the meaning of each water bowl, the number of bowls, the starting directions for setting and taking down the bowls, purification with incense, the gap of space between the bowls, the filled level of the water, and how I take down, clean, and dry the bowls. All these actions are done with certain intentions and recitations. I prepare my mind and intention before the offering begins. At the end of the day, I transfer the blessed offering of water from the altar to a new environment for respectful handling—I drain it in the sink, give it to birds, water plants, etc.

The water bowl offering describes the journey of the book and the writing path of my offering.

I practice the Tibetan Buddhist tradition on how to properly take care of the texts because the words help sentient beings to liberation. The texts are not to have direct contact on floors, chairs, and beds. I don't place cups, clothes, smartphones, for instance, on top of the texts. The soles of my feet do not face the direction of the texts. Texts are not discarded in rubbish bins; traditionally, pages are burned, though nowadays there is a burning law in my city. After a text or page falls on the floor by accident, sometimes I place it on the top of my head as an act of respect for the teachings that liberate sentient beings. These are some of the practices. I value the practices of respecting the texts and pages.

> How can I honor and respect the words, images, and content of the book?

The book has been harvesting and germinating.

I envision a ritual that comes with the birth/rebirth of the book. Seeds sprout or remain dormant until the conditions arise to grow. Germination. Dr. Funie Hsu says about recovery as Germination Pedagogy, "Compost the violence and the destruction and make it into something that's generative."

SEEDS offered lifelines for composting.

And now, I include notes from an email I sent on November 29, 2022 in response to when Clelia asked those in attendance the question should be treated as if the ancestors were asking it: "Harvesting, sharing the harvest, and knowing / nutrienting / microbing the soil before I can care for and bring seeds to be offered. Maybe planting the seed is after the October 2023 cycle."

Preparing the writing for my offering has been a spiritual journey. My seed has its own pace, timing, synchronicity, and spirit with the frequencies of human intentions and nature.

Knowledge germinates in relationship. I await the book, the seed, for continuing my writing that has a rebirth of its own.

*****

Yesterday was a good day for the seed gathering.

Yesterday was an auspicious day because of the Air-Air element combination. The Air-Air element combination is seen as the opener of the conditions for swift completion of projects or activities, and is very good for starting a path or spiritual practice.

Air is formless water. I breathe air . . . I breathe water. The Namib desert beetle harvests water from the air. Water is formless and form.

Water is creative, and reflective. I have been creating my seeds in the Water element year in the Buddhist and Asian lunar calendars.

Yesterday, I listened to the medicine shared by the voices for the book—Bones, Earth, and Water.

Yesterday was an auspicious day to gather.

I have a karmic relationship with the voices in this group that weave together again in this lifetime on the path towards Liberation. *How is it that I have come together with the voices in this group?*

My body can transition today, tomorrow, or next year. I don't know when my transition day is. My human rebirth is precious . . . and so, I am doing what I am doing. If I transition today, then I transition knowing that I had listened, shared, and received from this community. I am a seed and teaching in the making.

REFERENCES

Bucar, L. (2022, September 20). Religious appropriation depends on whiteness too. *Religion & Politics*. https://religionandpolitics.org/2022/09/20/religious-appropriation-depends-on-whiteness-too/

Hsu, F. (2022, November 16). *TheWonLab: Recovering the Asian American foundations of American Buddhism* WBS Learn [Video]. YouTube. https://www.youtube.com/watch?v=2G4vvvfA8Nc&t=2362s

Putcha, R. S. (2022, September 7). The ubiquity of religious appropriation, a review of "stealing my religion: Not just any cultural appropriation. *The Revealer*. https://therevealer.org/the-ubiquity-of-religious-appropriation/

13 Moons o o o o o o o o o o o o o

Danielle Denichaud

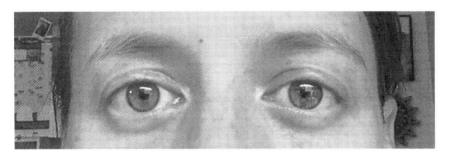

Menstrual cycles in 364 days
Unlucky—the missing floor
The card of death
An auspicious day
The 13th constellation I was born under—have you heard of the serpent bearer, Ophiuchus?
The day of my birth

My Offering

13 is gifted in reciprocity with an ancestral seed from El Salvador, offered to nourish the soil of the book *Who Are You Without Colonialism?: Pedagogies of Liberation (2023)* Edited by Clelia O. Rodríguez and Josephine Gabi; to you, I offer my humble gratitude for this collaborative birthing. This video was enliv-

ened on the Traditional Lands of my human relatives the Haudenosaunee, Anishinaabe, Huron-Wendat and Mississaugas of the Credit Peoples. Lands, where I have gratefully resided for seven years generally, and three years specifically, in the city known as Tkaronto/Toronto in the Bloorcourt district.

Why This, and Who Am I?

My life is a journey of being/sharing/witnessing/growing my felt sense as Earth child, Star child, female embodiment, child of parents born under the yoke of Afrikaner culture; mon père, Philippe, whose great great grandparents escaped religious persecution, and mia cara mama Yvonne, whose grandparents fled famine. I am an auto-immune dis-ease carrier who has perched on the precipice of my death, seeker and steward of life-sustaining healing arts, the ones tended by generations under patriarchal, colonial, mechanistic-rational siege. I have been blessed to breathe, sensate, dance, moan, imbibe, and braid myself back to life with languages of connection, regeneration and honouring. These arts are my medicines, re-membering my conscious identity of harmonious reciprocity with this young mind, ancient body, wise heart and cosmic soul, being/becoming/enlivened in irreducible interdependence with Earth and all Her Kin.

What Am I Sharing?

A movement, sound, text offering. A 13-minute journey; 13 tones of relationship I cultivate with my identity roots. These frequencies take shape through/as/in my embodied form, as a practice of weaving intentional threads into this tapestry of All Life i/we are welcomed to participate in. These languages resurrect me from the death currents of -isms, separations, hierarchies, cartesian silos and intergenerational colonial violence across time, place and space which inhabit me. They re-member me home to my Earthliness, Cosmicness, Humanness; where Life is nurtured and cherished by Natural Laws of symbiotic mutual thriving, regeneration, honouring and celebration of this Sacred Hoop of Life.

Invitations for Listening, Receiving, Beholding

Like sunrise, thunderstorm, waterfall, landslide, flocking, growing, transmutating, healing…this journey is layered and ecstatic, filled with unbridled creativity, presence, reflection and curiosity. Released from dams of propriety, expression bursts forth in abundance, celebrating this symphony of Life through a revelation of all that is present when mind, body, heart and spirit are welcomed to stoke the fire of my consciousness. In sharing these languages, I invite you to journey home with me, to our Earth bodies, of/on our Mother Earth's body, held within this Cosmic womb; may we be awakened to the numinous reality of being kin, to one another and all fellow Earth dwellers.

Scan to access or visit: https://vimeo.com/852391481/eed793450a?share=copy

Video Guide

1—entering—listening with maple—breathing
2—arriving—shaking—coughing from waste—mala beads passing through sandalwood
3—awakening spine with pine—iron ball
4—sensing—lungs—grief—sobbing—trust—laughing—air
5—discovering—kidneys—hu breath—fear of the mystery—inner trust—water
6—connecting—growling at saw—liver—discernment—rage turned holy—wood
7—creating—heart—dancing between apathy and joy—singing bowl—fire
8—naming—spleen—life force—love making with echinacea purpurea—earth
9—imagining—golden ball—gather, lift, expand, contract, allow, repel, balance, release – praying
10—integrating—release from the mind, heart, gut/womb—koshi elemental chimes water & fire
11—reflecting—bringing down the heavens—koshi elemental chimes air & earth—drinking water
12—concluding—riffing playfulness & defiant joy beneath the nauseating hum of electrical tower
13—exiting—honouring maple, grass, sky, cloud, sun, air, fire, water, earth, ether—breathing

My Pedagogical Roots (or, who has entrusted me to steward these practices)

The life-sustaining practices shared in this video—sound—movement—word offering have been gifted generously by my teachers to keep alive, embody deeply, and share lovingly. To you, I owe my hope, joy and perseverance; in naming you, I also intend to honour the lineage of teachers on your pathways back seven generations: Lorenna Bousquet-Kacera, Shantree Kacera and their teachers Joanna Macy, Brian Swimme, Thomas Berry, Stephen Harrod Buhner; Andrea Nann, her daughter & the Dreamwalker Core Ensemble; Donna Gates; Sage Walker and the Pathwork; Mother Earth and all of Her Earth kin who inspire me to bow in gratitude while asking how to walk well, in harmony & reciprocity, within this Sacred Hoop of Life.

I, Danielle Denichaud, am the composer of this current form of expression; I am not the creator of this offering. Its present form has been growing my entire embodied life, and so carries the imprint of every relationship with my Earth kin and walk through flowers, each tree climbed and lake swum, each cloud gazed and star sky dreamed to. My ancestors are present too. I may not know their names, but their songs live through me; calling me to dance beneath the moon and awaken early to pray with the sunrise on our Earth's horizon. They beckon me forward through the dark times, to sing into the storm and dance these feet into concrete until the path is cleared for Life to thrive again in joy and wonderment. I also honour the more-than-human communities that inhabit/enliven my fleshy, liquid, tendinous, bony terrain of this body home. These Earth kin, whom we call bacteria, viruses and fungi, are more numerous than human cells in my/your body; intimately dancing us into each functional, expressive, creative moment. What is their role in creating these thoughts, movements and sounds? And what of the soil, sun, water, air and spaciousness nurturing my body into existence since the beginning of this embodied Earth walk? They, too, are credited with the inspirations shared here within. Aho.

Without Colonialism I Am

Ram Trikha

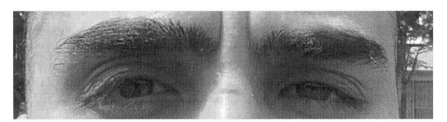

> Quem sou eu?
> Assustou-se tanto que parou
> completamente du pensar
> —In Clarice Lispector's *A Hora da Estrela.*

This question "who are you without colonialism?" has been dancing in my heart and mind since September 2022 when it was presented in the co-learning space of SEEDS for Change. I am on a journey still trying to answer this multi-layered and complex question.

Without Colonialism I Am:
A creator. An artist. A learner. A teacher. A listener. A storyteller. A writer. A being.
The universe experiencing itself.
I listen and look inwards. I create what I create, feeling the world around me.
In harmony with Mother Nature, I share the music that comes from my soul, as birds do.
Flowing along the river, basking gratefully in the sun, as the lotus does.

Who Are You Without Colonialism? Pedagogies of Liberation, pages 81–82.
Copyright © 2023 by Information Age Publishing
www.infoagepub.com
All rights of reproduction in any form reserved.

Being

I am water. The wave, arising out of oblivion, taking form for a glorious moment, and then returning to where I came from.

I am a human embodiment of the traits of Saraswati Mata's presence.

With colonialism, I am the same at my core. The difference is I face a myriad of hurdles before I can 'turn the corner and run into' myself.

In the present, I am in the process of way-finding, inspired by voices from the community, and voices from the culture.

The OGs lead me to freedom, and in turn, I strive to do my real job of freeing others.

Like many before me, I tend to seeds with Histories I know, seeds with love, and seeds with patience.

Fueling the fire where Truth resides, ensuring it stays protected.

With colonialism, if that means carrying the burden the way the Loon wound up with red eyes, then so be it.

I do my part.

To deal with the burdens of colonialism, I am one who lives by a code like the Mandalorian does. Or the Jedi.

Trying to keep my balance, with distractions all around me.

Redefining luxury, and my relationship with time.

I long for the feeling of being rid of the '-isms'. Undisturbed by noise, opinions and toxicity. At peace without the unnecessary turbulence, the unstable agitation, of Colonialist notions.

Until then, I must weather the storm and look to the stars to find my way.

Crawl, with the baton that my now-Ancestor Nipsey handed me.

Keep my heart pure as I chop wood and carry water.

I am still the lotus, the river, and the bird. I am still the universe experiencing itself.

I am who I am meant to be.

No matter how incessantly Colonialism and its many manifestations poke, gnaw, and stab at me, with the protection of my ancestors and my ancestors-in-the-making, I crawl.

REFERENCES

Hughes, L. (1995). Final curve. In A. Rampersad & D. Roessel (Eds.). *The collected works of Langston Hughes* (pp. 368–368). Vintage Books.

Lispector, C. (1977). *A hora da estrela*. Rosso.

Morrison, T. (1988). *Beloved*. Plume.

Wang, E. M. (2022, September 28). *Wayfinding as a way of being and knowing.* SEEDS for Change Series. https://www.seedsforchange.ca/learning-without-borders

The Body is an Altar Unaltered

Hope Kitts

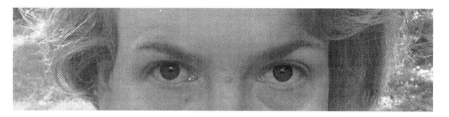

Without colonialism *my body* is for myself, not for the perception of myself.
It does not exist in relation to others' responses to it.
It is not a receding horizon of perfection, a lure for production.
It is not for sculpting, extracting or surveilling. No.
Rather, it *is the flesh of the cosmos* on loan.
It does not contain consciousness, it is consciousness.
It is not a means to an end. It is the end itself.
Sufficient. Sacred.

The thick hair that grows underneath my arms gets to stay;
more than that, it gets to feel the breeze whether anyone around me likes it or not.
My fuzzy legs glisten in the sun,
and my breasts show the gravity of a child's appetite.
No mouse-voice always in the form of a question,
my voice sinks low, it waits,
and is not responsible for anyone's feelings.

I meet others for the first time.
I do not resemble a horrid past that has never, can never, be made right.
I do not need to demonstrate my "wokeness."
I do not function to surveil, nor "ask to speak with the manager," nor expect comfort and validation everywhere.
I approach strangers without grief or apology, without wondering if I am secretly hated for the privileges I wish I could refuse.
Gone are the pathetic smiles that curl my mouth upward in attempts to connect, attempts to show I am "one of the good ones."
The white smile meant to signal camaraderie is unnecessary, because I know that a smile is not
compensation, it is condescension. It cannot substitute for reparations long overdue.
In its place the illusion of separateness is shattered, connection untainted.
The past, though acknowledged and understood, does not haunt our relation.
We are permitted the NOW together.

Without colonialism I am back in Brooklyn 16 years ago, unafraid of my feelings for Fred, not
affected to my depths by a 276-year ban on interracial marriage, and my (albeit liberal) grandmother's potential, unconscious, unwilling reaction.
I let our connection unfold. I see where it takes us, and I don't have to wonder what might have
been.
My children don't look like me.
Unlike my great-grandmother, I do not have to choose between my love and my citizenship, my
partner and my community.
I am not karmically in debt, having descended from "Eisenhower's rocket man."
My children learn the names John Brown, the Grimke sisters, William Lloyd Garrison, Anne
McCarty Braden, Viola Liuzzo.
Bravery, honor and courage are rooted in resistance.

Generational trauma does not live in my cells, does not bubble up with each feigned whine.
Rather than giving into the maternal rage that compels me to throw my child in the lake,
or strike him
or whip him, as I was whipped, as my dad and his dad were whipped—for the sake of "discipline," for the sake of desensitizing the oppressor consciousness to brutality—
I muster all of my strength to abstain, to observe my throbbing pulse without responding to it,
to break the cycle of abuse that is my only inheritance.

In those moments when I break through, I crack a little smile.
When I remember that it does not have to be this way, my vulva tingles shamelessly.

My body responds immediately to the promise of an alternative.
Water moves up my spine,
and my joy is not a threat to my conditioning.

I am not a consumer.
I am not scrolling to mimic belonging. I belong, unrelated to shared oppression or
> privilege.
I am present with my children without wanting to check my email, my shares, my
> likes.
I walk and drive and talk s-l-o-w-l-y, not self-conscious that I
> am taking too much time
> will be run off the road
> will be interrupted.
I am still.
"Efficiency" and "productivity" are dirty words, because time is never wasted.
I am not here to accomplish or to accrue.
Every experience is not a potential resume line, because
I am not in competition. I am in communion.
I am not toxically positive, nor do I expect others to be so.
The world is not my oyster. I cannot "do anything."
The sky IS the limit.
I have limits, and I have boundaries, and that is not a bad thing.
Boundaries are respected. Treaties unbroken.
In connection and expanding outward, beyond my own body, I am in ceremony.

I am small, enmeshed, not-separate.
I am not afraid of my own death, nor do I rush toward it with every waking mo-
> ment, wanting
> every beginning to be an ending, a box checked.
I have the human right to be housed, to breathe clean air, drink clean water, eat
> food that benefits
> the planet, to love my body–without having to ask permission; without a fee;
> without a mani and a pedi, a color and a cut, a quick shave and a nip and tuck;
> without a debt or the expectation of exchange.
I love myself as is, not as I want myself to be.
I love others as they are, not as I wish they were.
I challenge when necessary and because I love, unburdened by people-pleasing.
Without colonialism, there is no transaction, and I do not "keep the line moving."
I see that EVERYTHING is alive: The waves feel my heartbeat, the rocks know
> my soles, the
> winds check my ego.
The value of all things is intrinsic, interconnected:
A bud that cannot be rushed into blooming,
A sapling that takes only as much as it needs,
A river running its course.
And witnessing–without having to own, without needing to change–is enough.
Without colonialism our bodies are altars, unaltered.

Deadlines / Dead-Lines / Đét-Lai. Đét-Lai / Dead-Lines / Deadlines

Trung M. Nguyễn

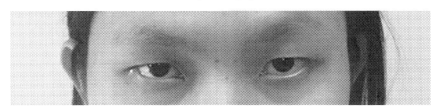

Tiếng Anh là ngôn ngữ toàn cầu, họ bảo vậy
nhưng là toàn cầu hoá với ai và phiên bản Anh ngữ nào, em không chắc
Em chỉ cảm thấy thật tồi tệ một khi nhìn thấu bản tính của deadline.
Deadline của ai và hắn muốn em rượt đuổi điều gì?

Là một học sĩ
em được mong đợi phải hướng dẫn người học cách quản lý thời gian và deadline.
Nhưng bản thân em vùng vẫy
trong chính hệ quy chiếu ấy
để bắt kịp deadline
Em phải dạy thế nào?
Liệu em có phải là một học sĩ, nhà giáo, người bạn, một nhà hoạt động cộng đồng
    tốt không?
Em cũng không biết nữa
Em sắm mình nhiều vai

mà thời gian lại hữu hạn
trên mảnh đất này

Thứ deadline mà em phải đối mặt rất đắt đỏ
Clelia O. Rodríguez từng tâm sự với em qua trang sách
    cái hội đồng đấy chẳng có quan tâm nếu bạn có internet đủ tốt hay không, hay tiền đâu mà bạn trang trải hội phí, điều mà có thì cũng chẳng đảm bảo bạn sẽ có đủ phí ăn uống hay di chuyển, vài hôm nữa trong tài3 khoản ngân hàng của bạn là phí thuộc địa bạn phải trả

Em đọc một mạch những câu từ đó
một hơi đủ sâu để người mẹ ở đất nước "Thế giới thứ ba" có thể nghe
bởi lẽ những câu chữ trên mang trong mình một thực tế
quay cuồng bởi dòng tiền tệ với tỷ giá cách xa phương Tây nhiều biển hồ sâu

Nghe đâu
Tại hội thảo nơi em dự
họ hay đàm đạo về chủ nghĩa thuộc địa thực dân
Kì thực họ nheo nhéo cụm từ như một xu hướng mới
Nhiều đề tài rào rào khắp nơi: phi thuộc địa hoá
nhưng thật có mấy người áp dụng những điều họ hô hào?
Trăm đô mỗi người
Nào là phát biểu về sự đa dạng, rồi lại cáo lỗi do vạ mồm

Sau bài thơ này
em lại trở về với những deadline
Deadline bảo Ariana, cô bạn học sĩ, một bà mẹ đơn thân, rằng cô làm chưa hết
    công suất
mặc cho bao chuyện phải lo toan
Deadline giục cô phải nộp hàng chục bộ hồ sơ xin tiền hỗ trợ
mông lung mà lại chẳng đảm bảo trợ cấp cho đứa con
Ella mệt mỏi
Ella ngỡ cô sẽ được tham dự trực tuyến để giảm chi phí
Hội thảo bảo Không!
Chúng tôi không cam kết được vì thiếu nguồn lực

Nguồn lực
là một nguồn căn của deadline
một nguyên cớ để chối bỏ hỗ trợ cho những cộng đồng cần giúp đỡ
Bạn không thể cãi lại những thể chế mang tính tư bản thuộc địa chiếm đóng
một khi họ đã nói họ không có nguồn lực
cắp được từ đây và đó đây
một khi bạn đã lỡ con deadline họ giao
Được kiến tạo nhưng không có Căn cứ
Lý lẽ của bọn họ
Thuốc súng của Kẻ chủ nô

Thi sĩ Juan de Dios Sánchez Jurado từng nói
    Ta không thể xúi một đoá hoa nở mau, một quả táo chớm rụng

Nên thơ!
Tại sao ta phải bị hối viết vội vài trăm trang luận cuối kì ở trường?
Ta học được gì từ hàng hàng những suy nghĩ bị thúc vội phải thấu ngay?
Công việc ở các hệ thống tập đoàn xử phạt người làm đi trễ trên từng phút
Nhưng sẵn sàng làm ngơ khi trả lương không đủ để sống cho nhân công
Deadline là một kiến tạo của kẻ cầm quyền và chẳng bao giờ thuộc về nhóm yếu
    thế
Bởi thế

Deadline là lằn ranh-chết
Vạch nơi mà lửa sự sống bị dập ngang
Người học, nhân công, người mẹ, đứa trẻ, những người lê lết trong tư bản,
phải luôn chân rượt đuổi khi bị cầm giữ bởi deadline
Tán cây, không khí, đại dương, muôn loài trên toàn thế giới
đang sinh tồn trên những lằn-chết vì sự thiếu hụt của *một* deadline

Khi những người yếu thế yêu cầu deadline, kẻ cầm quyền bảo Không!

Đét-lai
Một phiên bản Việt hoá từ căn gốc thực dân của deadline
Những người Việt làm công toàn cầu hiểu thứ từ mượn này rất rõ
Người mẹ, đứa trẻ, những người lê lết trong tư bản toàn cầu làm việc không ngừng
    nghỉ
tạo ra cái quần, cái áo, đồ điện tử, thức ăn, dịch vụ

sản-xuất-tại-Việt-Nam
sản-xuất-tại-Bangladesh
sản-xuất-tại-Thổ Nhĩ-Kì
sản-xuất-tại-Ấn-Độ
sản-xuất-tại-Cam-pu-chia
sản-xuất-tại-Trung-Quốc
Đúng! Họ đều hiểu thế nào là đét-lai
Nhiều người phải trả bằng mạng sống cho hiệu quả công suất của Các Nước Giàu

Tiếng Anh là ngôn ngữ toàn cầu, họ bảo
Toàn cầu *hoá*, em nhắc
của chế độ nô lệ thực dân

So...

Dạy deadline hay lằn-chết hay đét-lai theo một cách khác là phương pháp sư phạm
    mang tính giải phóng
Hiểu deadline theo cách khác đi là phương pháp sư phạm mang tính giải phóng
Thực hành deadline khác đi là phương pháp sư phạm mang tính giải phóng
Giao deadline khác đi là phương pháp sư phạm mang tính giải phóng
Cự deadline khác đi là phương pháp sư phạm mang tính giải phóng

Ta cần bắt đầu đâu đó
để học quên đi những công cụ Kẻ chủ nô đã găm vào đầu

bell hooks dạy em rằng

*Sự quan tâm và động viên, trái ngược lại bạo hành và xi và, mới là nguồn căn của
   yêu thương*
Em muốn bắt đầu với Sự quan tâm ấy

Còn bạn thì sao?
What would you do to free yourself from the chains of colonial deadlines?

Trích dẫn nguồn

Deadlines / Dead-Lines / Đét-Lai.

English is a global language, they say
but whose globalization and what English, I am not sure
I just know once I learned of the politics of deadlines, I am not happy
Whose deadlines and what is it that you want me to chase?

As a scholar
I am supposed to teach students how to manage time and deadlines
But I struggle
myself
within the system
how to keep deadlines
So how am I going to teach?
Am I a deserving student, teacher, scholar, friend, and community builder?
I don't know
I have many hats to wear
with so limited time to spend
on this land

The deadlines I'm facing are costly
Clelia O. Rodríguez told me vicariously in her book
   the committee doesn't really care if you have electricity a reliable internet
   connection or money to pay for the membership which doesn't guarantee you
   a spot lodging and travel arrangements colonial fees will be reflected in your
   bank account soon
I sigh all that sentence in one breath
so deep that my mother far in the Global South can hear
because every word spoke visceral reality
more so spiraling when your currency is somewhere oceans behind settler Wests

Though
at my kind of conferences
they do talk a lot about coloniality
In fact, it becomes a trend
Many CFPs sprinkled with *decolonization*
but will not commit to what they actually preach
even with hundreds of dollars paid each
the diversity speeches, the aftermath apologies

After writing this poem
I will come back to deadlines

Deadlines that told Ariana, my single-mother-scholar-friend she is not efficient
    enough
wearing as many hats as I do, or even more so
Deadlines that haunt her to apply for lists of unguaranteed funding
with no promises of childcare support
Ella is tired
Ella thought she could take a break by Zooming in
Conference said no!
We do not promise because of limited resource

Resource
is another causality of deadlines
another excuse for rejection of communities in need
You cannot argue with rampant imperialist settler-colonialist institutions
when they say they don't have resources
stolen from here and elsewhere
because you missed their deadlines
Founded but not Grounded
their rationale
Gunpowder of the Master

Poet Juan de Dios Sánchez Jurado once said
You cannot rush a flower to blossom, an apple to fall from tree

How beautiful!
Why were you rushed to submit that many final projects in school?
Did you learn anything by speeding up thoughts not in its time to grasp?
Corporate jobs that penalize when workers are late by minutes
but will ignore deadlines for when they must pay you livable wage

Deadlines are abstract set by the power and never the disenfranchised

Hence

Deadlines are dead-lines
or Lines at which living fires are extinguished
Students, workers, mothers, children, capitalist survivors,
constantly chase while held hostage by deadlines
Trees, air, oceans, non-human animals of the global climate
exist on dead-lines for a lack of the *real* deadlines

When the disenfranchised asks for deadlines, the power says no!

Đét-lai

a Vietnamized rendition of dead-lines from its colonizers
Global Vietnamese workers know this borrowed/enforced language very well
Mothers, children, global capitalist-survivors work tirelessly to their bones
for your clothes, devices, food, services

made-in-Vietnam
made-in-Bangladesh

made-in-Turkey
made-in-India
made-in-Cambodia
made-in-China

So yes! They do know dét-lai
Many paid lives to productivity of the Global North

English is a global language, they say
Global*ized*, I add,
of the colonizers

Vậy nên...

To teach deadlines or dead-lines or dét-lai differently is a liberatory pedagogy
To understand deadlines differently is a liberatory pedagogy
To practice deadlines differently is a liberatory pedagogy
To assign deadlines differently is a liberatory pedagogy
To resist deadlines differently is a liberatory pedagogy

We must all start somewhere
to unlearn tools of the Masters

bell hooks taught me
    Care and affirmation, the opposite of abuse and humiliation, are the foundation of love
Tôi want to start with *Care*.

REFERENCES

Anzaldúa, G. (2015). Speaking in tTongues: The third world women writers. In C. Moraga, & G. Anzaldúa (Eds.), *This bridge called my back: Writings by radical women of color*. (4th ed., 161–172). SUNY Press.

Berenice, A. (2023, January 19). My wishes for the decolonization of global health. *Mamá Chingona Diary*. My wishes for the decolonization of global health—Mamá Chingona Diary (wordpress.com)

hooks, b. (2000). *All about love: new visions*. William Morrow.

Mohanty, C. T. (2003). "Under western eyes" revisited: Feminist solidarity through anti-capitalist struggles. *Signs: Journal of Women in culture and Society*, 28(2), 499–535. https://doi.org/10.1086/342914

Rodríguez, C. O. (2018). *Decolonizing aAcademia: pPoverty, oOppression and Ppain*. Fernwood Publishing.

Sanchez Jury, J. D. (2012, August 12). Aparatico de yYoga. *Apetitosustituto*. APPETITE SUBSTITUTE: YOGA DEVICE (apetitosustituto.blogspot.com)

Qué sería yo y este mundo sin la Colonización

Odaymar Cuesta

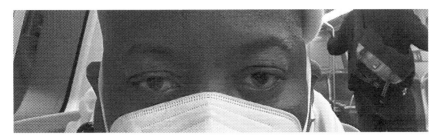

Primero que todo, Yo no sería Yo,
Seríamos personas en manera distinta

La Humanidad sería una cualidad valorada, inherente en el ADN
cuidarnos más allá de la pertenencia al clan, a la familia y amistades
cuidarnos, tener valor, amor, cuidarnos por podemos, porque queremos
desde el día uno de la historia hacer la historia.

Con verdad, conocimiento en ancestrología, creencias, fe, religiosidades,
cosmovisión tan repleta, tan completa, convivencia con y en otros planetas.

Asimilando e incorporando la libertad, de vivir sin traumas, sin dolor, sin venganzas
sin muertes, sin resentimientos.

Vivir y crecer sin colonialismo taladrándote tu mente, corroyendo el alma, secando
   los sueños, condenando tu existencia misma.

Vivir y crecer sin asco, esa náusea al levantarse cada día y presenciar tanta injusticia, tanta colonia, respirar tanta muerte y silencio, tanta torpeza, tantos contaminantes.

¿Qué sería yo sin la COLONización? Desmantelar todo lo que conocemos, a lo que estamos habituados, desestabilizar las memorias, nuestra vida toda, interrogando mi descendencia, mis elucubraciones, interrumpiendo el propósito del ahora,
cuestionar no termina, no reposa, no descansa.

Sin la colonización, sin esclavitud, el mercadeo humano, sin la white supremacy, sin las supremacías, lo blanco, sin esa necesidad enfermiza de vigilancia de control, de extermino de conquista, de subyugación.

¿Qué seríamos? No creo tener respuesta a tan inmensa pregunta
Esto es una interpretación ficcional de donde me lleve mi mente y mis pensamientos 5 a 7 siglos en retorcería y empezar de nuevo empezar de cero, empezar primero.

De 5 a 7 siglos de recuperación de memoria, liberación, acuñar, confortar a la tierra, la comunidad/corazón.

Solo de imaginarlo lágrimas llenan mis ojos, es como estar en el presente hacia el futuro teniendo que habitar el pasado para armarnos para desplegar, la labor de amor, la estrategia política la reconstrucción la anticipación.

De la Liberación, la perpetuidad del goce, del descanso, del existir, del habitar en expansión, alineados con los ciclos de la tierra, trabajando en equipo siendo equipos

La colonización nos ha quitado todo y nos ha dado todo,
la colonización nos ha denominado negros, blancos, indígenas, mujeres, hombres, Cisgéneros, transgéneros, heterosexuales, bisexuales, queers, sanos, enfermos, ricos, pobres.

Nos han encasillado, enjaulado, restringido en binarismos simplistas, coaptado, condicionado, transformado, violado una y otra vez nuestra condición, la sanción, salvación y recuperación de nosotros , la oportunidad de ser nuestro destino de viajar hacia nosotros, de ser nosotros, ha sido y será un proceso profundo de exterminio masivo, masacre colectiva con tiempo ilimitado.

Darnos la posibilidad de educarnos liberatoriamente es vital para enseñar un mundo descolonizado, un acercamiento especulativo a la realidad, la imaginación y el poder que emana de ella es clave pa liberarnos, pa hacer realidad nuestros sueños.

Poder equilibrar la verdadera línea vital, con la real edad de nuestros souls quitándole el cansancio la penuria y la dureza que significa existir, sin Colonización seríamos eternos, el planeta estaría irreconocible.

Yo, myself, and I descansade, descansada, descansado, saludable y feliz
En placer en gratitud, lejos de la tecnología y labor productiva
lo que conocemos por jornada de esclavización de 8 horas y más, será un recuerdo borroso de las historias de nuestros antepasados

Alíen (2023). 9 x 12. Acrílico en lienzo.

la producción de contenido y los influencer, esa necesidad de relacionarse, esa herramienta moderna y colonialista, obsoleta y olvidada a la misma vez
las fronteras y países, vecinos familia con acceso a visitarnos a intercambiar
nadie conquista nada, ni divide
nadie explota nadie, ni mata
nada es superior a nadie, sin ego
nadie tiene valor por nada o por algo
algo siempre se aprecia, se retribuye
Todo se comparte, se comparte

No se espera, se hace, se construye
ImaginationRealityImaginationReality Imaginación Realidad

Despertarnos mañana 26 de julio liberados, renovados, vividos
Como debió de ser siempre, despertarnos sin COLON que nos joda la vida
el COLON español, conquistador y COLON el órgano que acumula y guarda la tristeza, pérdida y miedo recuperado, sanado, sin doler,
constantemente sin podrirse de tanto aguantar de tanto maniobrar
amargo tragar.
Sin colonialismo mi trabajo
no tendría sentido, ni muchos trabajos que se hacen,
inclusive este escrito no tuviera razón de existir
porque seríamos plenas criaturas en posesión de libertad, respeto, gratitud, humildad y todas esas cualidades que el colonialismo quiere quitarnos, quiere ripiarnos

Qué maravilla sin tener que estar alerta, ni tener el sistema nervioso tan desgastado, tan roto y destrozado

Colonialismo sería una mera palabra obsoleta del pasado
una palabra que nadie recordaría
ni su significado
¿estaríamos listos para eso?

¿Estaríamos dispuestos al cambio?
¿Cómo imaginar vivir sin algo que existe antes que yo? ¿Cómo desenmantelarlo? ¿Cómo desestabilizarlo? ¿Cuál estrategia seguir? ¿Cuáles planes? ¿Cuál agenda?

Rezo, meditación, rituales que apuntan a la existencia
Prayer
You are here
You are sacred
We are not the first
We are not not the only ones
We are not the last
We are together
We are sacred
We are a force of change
We are medicine from the past present and future
Estamos aquí y
Tú eres sagrada sagrade sagrado
No somos ni los primeros ni los únicos ni los últimos
Nosotros estamos juntes y somos sagrados
Nosotros somos una fuerza de cambio
Nosotros somos medicina del pasado del presente y del futuro
We are not a curse
You are not damaged
We are not the problem

Qué sería yo y este mundo sin la Colonización • **97**

You are not too much
We are not evil we are not the devil

No estamos malditos
No estamos dañados
Nosotros no somos el problema
Nosotros no somos demasiado
Nosotros no somos diabólicos ni el diablo

We are expansive beings
Somos fluidity, somos future.

Unrooting the Colonial Seed

Karthik Vigneswaran

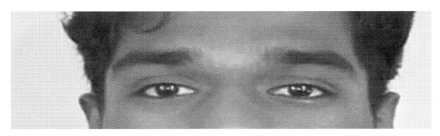

My name is Karthik and I call Canada home. My parents, Pushparany Vigneswaran and Vigneswaran Ganesh, left their home in Sri Lanka because of the war waged against our Tamil identity. I learned how to write Tamil in Canada with pencil and paper, whereas my parents learned it by running their fingers through soil. Coming from an ancestral lineage of farmers, my parents and ancestors all recognized themselves with the Land that gives us life. The Land we live among and get everything from, including our identity. My father often told me that we were '*mun-neram*' which in English translates to coloured soil because of the dark skin we have.

Teaching is the facilitation of one of the most beautiful processes of being alive—learning! I like to believe that as my mother sowed seeds with my grandfather to yield the crops the village needed my work, as a teacher is to work with those before me, and those after me, to sow the seeds of Knowledge that our

---

Who Are You Without Colonialism? Pedagogies of Liberation, pages 99–101.
Copyright © 2023 by Information Age Publishing
www.infoagepub.com
All rights of reproduction in any form reserved.

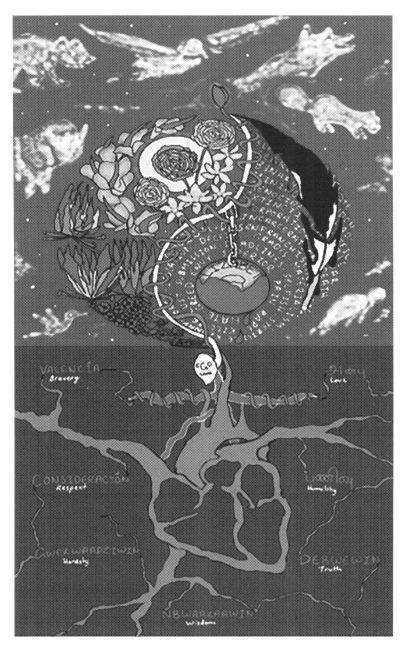

Unrooting the Colonial Seed. (2022) 2500 x 5000 (pixels), 2.1 mb, 96 dpi and 24 bits. I initially printed the piece, original size, onto an organic bamboo cotton clothing (6ft x 1 ft).

community needs. The teachers, who nourished my own learning growing up, did so by instilling land-based teachings. Teaching is political action, as Indigenous peoples and stewards of ancestral Knowledge remind us of daily.

Truth be told; I do not know who I am without colonialism. Words leave me when I hear the question. As I look within, I find values that support the dominant Western colonial system in place. I remind myself that the antidote is to unlearn. I have learned that decolonization is a political activity and that all teachers play a role within. To teach politically, I have to know the ancestral seeds I sow: Seeds of Love, Respect, and Compassion for all. In the process of unlearning colonial values, I have come across the Seven Teaching Principles of the Anishinabek People—teachings and values from Turtle Island. In the same way, Tamil people view the land as part of us, Indigenous peoples in Canada also view this land with Respect. When we hurt the land, we hurt ourselves. When we mutilate the land, we mutilate ourselves. When we love the land, we love ourselves. When we learn about the land, we learn about ourselves.

The experience of lacking words turned into questions that I visualized in my art piece I call, *Unrooting the Colonial Seed*. The drawing is my learning statement inspired by Dr. Rodríguez's offerings in her teachings on decolonizing work. A statement I now use to inspire my teaching and to focus on land-based Indigenous values. By re-focusing on them, I bring myself back to *that* land. Bring my students back to *that* land. My parents carry the honour of knowing and respecting the land. As farmers, they cared for the village planting what was only needed. What my *village* needs now, is a way to find itself back to *that* land.

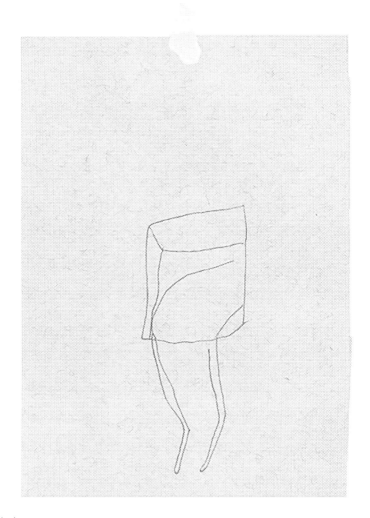

Untitled (2023)

▮▮▮ Root, ▮▮▮
▮▮

Shadow-Work as Pedagogical Training

Zahra Komeylian

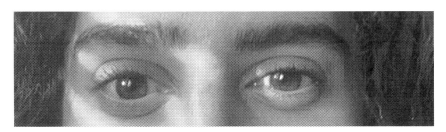

The drawings in this chapter were created through an inquiry of inner wounds (2022–2023). In our editorial process, Dr. Clelia O. Rodríguez presented me with the riddle to imagine myself outside my wounds through the act of redaction, in order to answer the question, **Who am I without colonialism**. As I redact the text where my personhood orients to the "master's narrative," I witness a self emerge that is conscious of the shadow but not bound by it. I write about these drawings to liberate them. What remains is a pedagogical record.

▮▮▮ I am the body of a black walnut tree. A wind blows and the tree remains fixed in its muddy soil deep in the ocean. My trunk is wide and has many rings. The first ten rings are ▮▮, then pulling apart, bowing, conflict, and incubation. My tall stature is my dignity. My branches yield

---

Who Are You Without Colonialism? Pedagogies of Liberation, pages 103–113.
Copyright © 2023 by Information Age Publishing
www.infoagepub.com
All rights of reproduction in any form reserved.

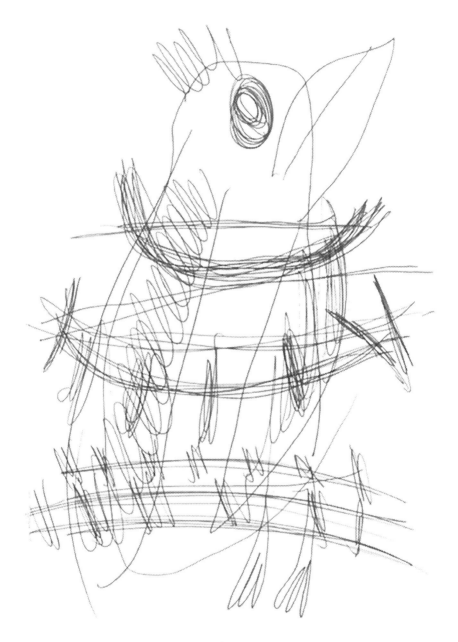

Brother's Rooster (2022)

Tracing the Root, Unearthing the Wound • **105**

Green Rooster, Black Rooster (2022)

Descending in Sainthood (2022)

Tracing the Root, Unearthing the Wound • 107

to the weight of green knots of knowing that gestate wisdom in the dark. I am not after the promise of arrival. I am the living link between past and present. ▮▮▮ the mulberries guide me. I know my mother. ▮▮▮

I am a root; I am not a phantom limb. Now, I can write, and my mind does not get lost in the innate lengthiness of Persian prose. Without colonialism, the liberation of my voice does not depend inherently on the stifling of an*other*'s.

I enter the forest. I ask it to show me a place inside myself that exists without these constructs. Lex asks me to think about the first woman who lived. ▮▮▮

In the forest, I see the sumac plants whose July berries are just turning red. Their stalks and the back of their leaves are soft like a sitting animal that I stroke. On one branch, the old fruit hanging dead from the past winter, and those just emerging into life are afforded a space to be. I am a quiet witness to the cycles of fertility and disintegration. The profound order that encompasses all things also contains me. In the presence of the Great Mother, exiled parts of me surface and take rest— whole and breathing. The sumacs become the anchor. They tell me my name, and they say, go *very slowly*. I breathe into my pain body. A knot releases. I know these velvet fruits from elsewhere. I am responsible to them, for they liberate me, they tell me who I am, and they stitch me back together.

▮▮▮ present ▮▮▮ I ▮▮▮ are narrated constellations of knowledge that are buried inside me ▮▮▮ Most of these drawings are larger than the size of my body. They are responses to questions from the *felt* place: I sit on the paper, and my hands divulge something from a place deeper than my lifespan.

▮▮▮ hundreds of ▮▮▮ sketches I have created ▮▮▮ ▮▮▮. Carrying symbols of kinship, wounding, and metamorphosis, they emerge from a period of visual self-inquiry and shadow work. In my process of creation, a web of women around me—my teachers and co-companions—have borne a sacred space to witness these works. From this web, my drawings have initiated me into my pedagogy.

I practice a pedagogy of creative self-inquiry. Pedagogy of the inner child, of the body, of creative synthesis—pedagogy of, "where is your heart?" Of slowness, of community, of—check in with one another. Pedagogy of gentleness. Honouring life. A pedagogy that makes it safe enough for students to come out from the shield of their phones. Of *feeling*.

███████████████████many times██████ in front of the classroom noticing my inner adolescent self and my inner ██████████ father—both emerging ██████ ████████████████████████████████████. And all the while, my students drink the elixir ████████████████████████████ ██████ hearing, "I ██████ have time to help you ██████ now" ████████████████████████████████

I returned home██████████████████ ████████████████

My wounds: ██ witnessed, ██ tended, ████████████████████████ ██ ██ container of myself. I returned to my pedagogical research, asking how I can keep myself alive while doing this work. Beyond the ████████████████████████, beyond the shadow of collective ██████████? There was ██ anchor, ██ there was a whisper. The whisper was a scribble, a messy sketch.

I start from the messy sketch; I confront the rooster that was stolen from me (see *Brother's Rooster,* 2022, *and Black Rooster, Green Rooster,* 2022). I confront the name of the father, and all that it concealed. The daughter, I, who had rendered her body erased to become a protective canopy for my father, my uncle, my cousin, the unearthed wounds (see *Descending into Sainthood*, 2022). I witness you, for we are all knotted together—and we begin to untether. In that, there is space to reclaim myself. I reclaim her from the layers that give me padding, trap me within, protect, and violate, force, incubate, silence. The daughter, I, sees the father in her belly (see *Sheep*, 2023). The father shrinks into a fetal position, the daughter, I, returns his wounds to him. She pushes him out as she pulls herself up into a verticality that is me. She reclaims herself from the bottleneck. Her arms return to her.

In a dream image, (see *Steeping,* 2023), she, I, confront a woman who sits ancient and solid like a sphinx in a bath and will not look at me. The woman is the emerging inner feminine/yin/anima; her growth terrifies the ego, but nonetheless, she grows.

Over time, the gestures of the bodies in these drawings have become more emphatic as they have begun to hold emergent intensities. Fragmented knowledge surfaces and is contained outside the body; constituent wounds slowly dissolve, releasing potentials for presence, relationality, and pedagogical dissent. Gradually, the grandness of the father shrinks on the paper (refer to *Descending into Sainthood*, 2022 and *Sheep*, 2023).

I conceive the pedagogue's journey as synonymous with the journey of the wounded healer or the shamanic journey (Anzaldúa, 2015). I cannot practice emancipatory pedagogy without having freed myself from what is buried within myself. Through the process of self-inquiry and drawing, a *me*search process, I nurture a space to return to my genealogy, the roots ▇▇▇▇▇▇▇▇, to go beyond myself (Douglas, 2017).

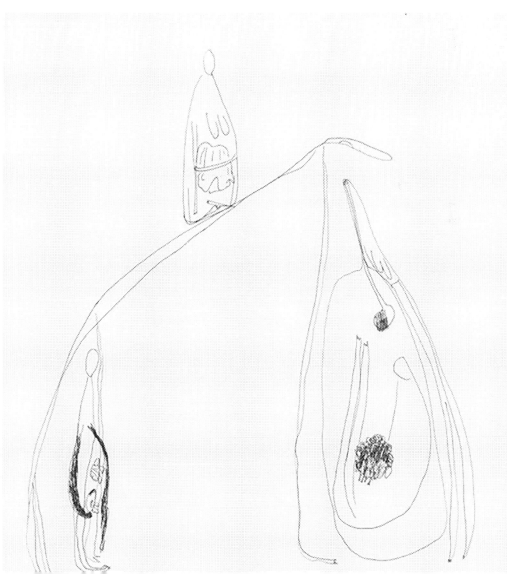

In dialogue with my inner images, the myth of my life, shared symbols of our collective stories, and our folklore, (Anzaldúa, 2009), I touch the source of embodied truth. Sitting by the primordial waters of the personal and collective unconscious, on the place preceding and beyond ███████████████████ ███████████████, I reach in with my hands and bring back some images. Even as they appear in glimpses, they shape me into an *imperfect whole,* mending the ███████ *self.* They slowly guide me to a time before the subjugation that closed the throat of woman.

Gloria Anzaldúa underlines that images *bridge* emotion and conscious knowledge and are more intimate with the unconscious than words (2009). Inquiring into my own shadow depths through the symbolic, I make space to see/listen/teach beyond binary modes of living (Anzaldúa, 1987; Kimmerer, 2013; Rodríguez, 2018). Creative self-inquiry grants me potential to break with a binary worldview. I reach into my shadow; I open space for my students to hold their own darkness.

> In a sort-of-inverted well, the living daughter and the unborn daughter are contorted between the mother's body, and the architectures of the well rock which seems to have no opening (see Well Water, 2023).

I—my sister—the woman who carried a woman—we scream. A million women are screaming. We reverberate in the deepest ring in the body of the walnut tree. Their screams render the body visible. This voice is me.

Swimming in these waters, I must touch the ruptures that are interweaved in my lineage. The moments ██████████████████, and truth █████████ in the shadow. Jafar, Ali, Ahmad, Soltan. The roots of my pain body.

Like the mulberries, the sumac, the walnut tree, the body gives a direction and holds a way to keep living. On the paper, the water makes a mark, to a site to keep returning to. My grandmother's tears drop into the water. I turn to her ████ ██ █████ I run █████, I am ███████████████████████ I have inherited, I become with ██ limbs █████████████.

I turn to the wholeness of my students. I begin to play. My patience is softer. I am able to hold their anger. I don't scare so easily. Days ago, my student (my teacher), Chloe Gillard, writes to me, telling me that they have come across the names of nature, the name of cosmic consciousness, Aluna, from the teachings of the Kogi people. Chloe tells me that Aluna needs the human mind to participate in the world, because the thing about a human mind is that it is in a body.

Much of the violence we enact stems from our own profound state of fragmentation. Tracing the roots of our wounds, and then conceiving what we are without them is essential to the work of decolonization, which as indigenous scholarship emphasizes, demands an act of making whole that which has been broken (Anzaldúa, 1987; Kimmerer, 2013; Rodríguez, 2018). To mend this fragmentation, root work involves a slow writhing into the earth to protect and incubate the vulnerable self while uncovering the buried, feminine unconscious. I reflect

Steeping (2023)

Well Water

on the earthworm. For Woodman (1992) and Anzaldúa (2015), earth elementally represents the return to the feminine and an accessing and uncovering of the dark parts of the self. In this place, "She can honour her own blood, the passionate red that connects her to the moon above and the mud below.. This is the Great Mother alive–the creative matrix in which death is *constantly giving birth to life"* (Woodman, 1997, p. 18, emphasis added).

With my students, we go to the river. We have been meditating on how we can make intimacy with other living things based on the teachings of Leanne Simpson (Simpson, 2021; Simpson & Philip, 2020). We walk to the Don, yearning for closeness. On the sand, we draw concentric circles that show the distance we feel from all the aspects of nature. We start telling the river our stories.

The river, we know, became sick because we do not know it by its names. How can I love something I do not understand? A student places a dry branch at the centre of the concentric circles. The stick falls. All of the circles are now connected. And on the water, we see small circles appear and dissolve like the river telling us its ephemeral fingerprints. Chloe says the river teaches it is our work to learn nature by its true names. A silence falls over us. My name is walnut tree.

REFERENCES

Anzaldúa, G. E. (1987). *Borderlands/La frontera: The new Mestiza*. Aunt Lute Books.
Anzaldúa, G. (2009). *The Gloria Anzaldúa reader* (A. L. Keating, Ed.). Duke University Press.
Anzaldúa, G. (2015). *Light in the dark/luz en lo oscuro: Rewriting identity, spirituality, reality* (A. Keating, Ed.). Duke University Press.
Douglas, T. (2017). My reasonable response: Activating research, mesearch, wesearch to build systems of healing. *Critical Education, 8*(2), 21–30.
Kimmerer, R. W. (2013). *Braiding sweetgrass*. Milkweed Editions.
Mayes, C. (2005). The teacher as shaman. *Journal of Curriculum Studies, 37*(3), 329–348.
Rodríguez, C. O. (2018). *Decolonizing academia: Poverty, oppression and pain*. Fernwood Publishing.
Simpson, L. B. (2021). *A short history of the blockade: Giant beavers, diplomacy, and regeneration in Nishbaabewin*. CLC Kreisel Lecture Series. University of Alberta Press.
Simpson, L. B. & Philip, N. (2020). *Ga(s)p: Writing as reparative care* [Video]. Contingencies of Care Residency Program. YouTube. https://www.youtube.com/watch?v=B3w_hwAhQd8
Woodman, M. (1992). *Leaving my father's house: A journey to conscious femininity*. Shambhala.

without colonialism

Aquib Shaheed Yacoob

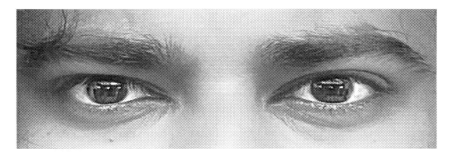

Grounded, inside my body. Clean, crawling. Curious.
I am me—*en route* to a journey I sit in at 30, but instead at 3.
United: with the people. family. gods of land, earth, skies and Allah. Vishnu. Christ.

                                                  my grandmother's child.

I live in my bold truths: accept *me* as fact and not declarations. honest answers about who

                                                          I love,
                                                        & loves me.

    How I worship, and feel.
Looking into the mirror—I hold the cracks and flowers, weeds and life that grow out of my fragments:

without colonialism • 117

    my blood, bones and body—free.

    embraced, not shamed.

    understood and seen.

out-side of any bi-a n-ar-y.

I floated through the catacombs today: below the Church.

                          where they raped our sacred connection.

                                     From the Earth,

                                   An extension of our

B   O   D   Y

                where they took our languages,

                        mother

t   o   n   g   u   e

                where they made *sodomites* of <u>our</u>

                      father's magic

                forced their <u>purity</u>

                      on <u>our</u>

w   h   o   l   e   ness

Who am I *without colonialism?*
free.

                                                                        me.
                                                                    magic.
                                                                      holy.
                                                                   whole.
                                                             abundant.
                                                             Grounded.

June 2019.
New York to Guyana.
(47,000 ft, unedited)

I think often that it's the transcripts of the past that hold the answers to the future. Digging deep into the mountains and oceans, I search for wisdom. And there it lives; and right before my own eyes—also. In my hands and veins; in my bones and gentle fingerprints. Stories of the past, present, future, and not-yet-known.

Allowing me to truly sit and listen to my bones—feel the blood that once coursed through my *nannies*. Listen, feel, and you'll learn the past. Trust deeply.

There is fear and blockage. So much. So so so much. That's part of the story. Part of the history: un-accessed for so so so long. Large clouds of *energy* and love and fears and desires and givings and takings and wantings and cravings and love. Peace. Harmony. Destruction. So much of that. Destruction. And finding.

Is that why I haven't listened? Because it was easier to look forward. To be only in the now. To think of tomorrow because yesterday was so so so very… everything.

I sit, with deep breaths, Raising my chest. Dropping. Life. I sit, and I look at my friend, my heart. Inwards. I feel the blood—our blood—that she pumps. That we pump. It's exhilarating.

My heart feels like I can't contain it. Like it wants to explode from the… everything. My fingers weak as I listen to the dance—the song—of my blood. Life. Flowing. Moving. Still.

Light panic sets in. "*But remember*, picknee*, you, we are in control. You stand with all of us.*" Together, listening. When I sit listening, I listen with the ferocity of all my kin. Leading the charge—*me*. Holding behind me, *us*. One and the same.

Together, I remember, I access, I feel, for us. The remembering, the accessing, the feeling we didn't do.

Pent up, all this *energy*. Repressed so so so deep so that we can't move. But a weight on our souls. One that must be lifted. For all of us—our Lives.

For *Nani*. For *Ajee*. For Me. For *Nana* and *Anja*. For Grandma and Grandpa. For mammie and daddie. For the rocks and the water and earth and the very air that 47,000 feet above carries us.

Yea—for the Wallmapu

I learn the thing I encounter and live the lives I lead for *purpose*. being. Each encounter, chanced and planned, takes me towards **wholeness**.

without colonialism, I am as free at "*tree*" as I am at thirty.
connected. grounded. beautiful chaos.
plenty.

Remnants of the In-Between

Anthazia Kadir

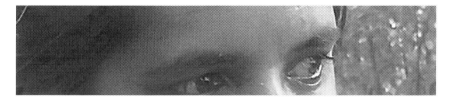

Remnants of the In-Between

Amidst temporal landscapes
Saturated with the sins of empire.

Clutching to the remnants -
bitter, fermented, and sour

I hear my ancestors
whispering.

Fragmented, my body sedated -
from the weight of the Saviour's scorn
Journeys;
Re-turning and homecoming

In these Caribbean spaces, where saltwater
meets the crevices of my pain.

Lingering Between my shadows
Trauma dripping from familiar
faces, memories
that will not leave me
alone.

Temporal Shorelines, rank with
forbidden nostalgia,

Bodies and Souls intermingling,
With rootedness, exile, and forbidden peace

BlaC Altar

Kay Williams

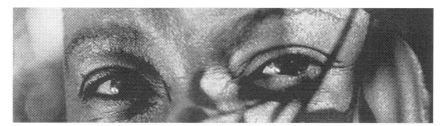

I am a free flowing, shape-shifting wielder of the elements. I am a diviner. I am a listener of divinity, closely and deeply with my ancestors. I am present in listening to my spiritual guides, the earth, elders, and in the teachings of every living being. **I am a re-memberer**. I rejoice in the re-joining with my ancestors and the primordial forces manifesting through nature. **Re-membering** is the constant work that claims what is beyond the umbral which predates colonialism—the light of my ancestry. This question, who am I without colonialism? is engaging me to reflect on my own practice to being able to respond (be response-able) to the visionary possibility of my own re-membrance over and over again. This question is a seed in bloom with origins in the unceded lands of the Lenka, the Chorti-Maya and the Nawat Peoples as part of a political pedagogical initiative grounded in Indigenous Knowledge.

Who am I without colonialism? I am in deep re-membrance of my place among my **Egúngún**, the collective name of my ancestors according to the indigenous knowledge system of the Yorùbá people of Yorùbá Land. I am the commitment to them to move with an ethic of **BlaC**

Who Are You Without Colonialism? Pedagogies of Liberation, pages 123–130.
Copyright © 2023 by Information Age Publishing
www.infoagepub.com
All rights of reproduction in any form reserved.

BlaC Love and Care (BLaC) is part of my cadre of world-building liberatory practices that support my understanding and growth in the communities and worlds I currently occupy, and the worlds I believe are yet to be (Williams, 2023). The **BLaC** Ethic is a recurring locale. I am the place where **BLaC** happens and the **BLaC** Ethic exists in the possibility of every place that my ancestors reside in the "I" that is me. I am continually shaping myself and being shaped by the ancestral me that recurs when I am intentionally re-membering with my lineage and rejecting where I am seduced to practice my own dismemberment. This Ethic is my social practice that centers the vastness of what is possible when the needs, dreams and abundance of my indigenous African ancestors and their descendants are tended to and affirmed with hope born out of political intentions.

My BlaC Altar

Love:
Care:
Relationships:
Collective Liberation:
of the Descendants of Indigenous African peoples:

movement:
response-Ability as possibility:
in action:
in the community:
to create visionary possibilities:

giver:
overflow:
tending to my raggedy:
healing:
abundance:

Blackness as technology:
Blackness as a whole:
birth:
innovations (Williams, 2021).
I am a being who rhythmically repeats myself in writing praxis.
I am cadence.
I am continuity.
I am a ritual altar builder.
I am a listener of grief…
I am the opener of ritual conversations…
I am a questioner…
I am a prayer, "help me"…

Ancestors:
"Help me, hear my heart, and help me to try to express who I am without colonialism in a way that can be heard!"

I beseech. I feel flustered by the nagging sense of inadequacy this question has come to generate in me. And so, I go to my ancestor's altar and I sing, I chant, I light a candle, I offer sacred smoke and I offer honey, Wray, and Nephews white rum to conjure their spirits:

"Ancestors: Help me, hear my heart, and help me to try to express who I am without colonialism in a way that can be heard!"

I beseech. Am I challenged to produce *the* answer? Do I owe it to myself? To my Indigenous African ancestors? "Help me, hear my heart, and help me to try to express who I am without colonialism in a way that can be heard!"

Aha!
I hear them gently
I hear their guide
I hear the divinatory sounds: "collaboration."
I pull cards.

First card asks: "What do you desire?" (Virtue, 2006)
I answered: I don't see the relevance.
I asked: How deep is my political yearning for an answer?

I am a wonderer…
Is this a feeling of envy for those who seem to know the answer?
Is my presumed lack of ties to land-based knowing why I don't seem to have a clear answer?

I fantasize
about what it might be like to know exactly where it is that one's people are "from"
about what it might be like to know who one's people are
about the names in which they know you and you know them.

I am a griever
I often sit with my relationship to this grief
I cannot know in what way I am with or without colonialism

I am a speaker
I sit and talk with my ancestors
who by their Yorùbá name are my Egúngún.
They know my names in my original languages even if I don't know theirs beyond knowing them as Egúngún in the Yorùbá language of the people of Yorùbá Land and their indigenous religion. "Ancestors: Help me, hear my heart, and help me to try to express who I am without colonialism in a way that can be heard!"

I am a reader
I get it. I understand why this card was their answer to my prayer.
"Return to your most tender self!"

Second card revealed itself, no shuffling required:
acceptance and letting go are the only solutions
no resolutions
or
repairs are possible (McGregor, 2018)

an old wound is preventing my balance

I am a feeler of deep grief
I sense and my breath… is taken away… for a moment…
I sit with the nuance of my violent location as a settler without nuance.
It is this grief,
my old wound, the impact of anti-blackness
that leaves me feeling in-between spaces of complex entanglements,
at a crossroads to occupy space in the conversation of what and who
becomes possible without it.

I reach the **BlaC Altar**
the echoes and ethos of my Egúngún
their sonorous frequencies
their nourishment to sustain me
their nesting

Third card announces a death
something that is ending
it has questions many questions: "how do you honor the mystery of life?", "what are you not valuing?", "how do you honor your energy?, "how do you engage with questions of blood?", "of forced settlements"
Ancestors remind me: Death is part of Life.

BlaC Altar

It is *here* that I re-member myself,

I re-member my commitment to how I sur/render to live through my own dying process.

It is *here* that I re-member what it means to "go out like a fucking meteor" as Audre Lorde in a *Burst of Light* exclaimed.

It is *here* that I am returned back to myself as a madquestionasking steward of **BlaC** love and Care.

It is *here* that I recognize that perhaps what needs to end for me is centering the colonialism part of the question of who I am without colonialism.

It is *here* perhaps where I center my present and imagination.

It is *here* perhaps in my truest form who I am without colonialism also exists in who I am with it.

It is *here* perhaps where I honor my time, where I honor Blackness, **BlaC** Love and Care.

This final card brings the generosity of my Egúngún: *Here* I am told that spiritual connection and healing is what is mostly needed. *Here* I am told that before I highlight people's unconscious issues I am to understand my own.

Here I am reminded and re-membered to go gently.. I am reminded of this re-membering through this card's message to me.

Deep breaths.

BlaC Altar

I rest my gaze and I see
My pottery,
Mother Earth is present,
The pottery is the vessel that holds the elements.
I returned to the question of "what do I desire?"
I desire that my work be received by those who have the heart to hold it
I am deep and abiding in love.
I am in deep conversation with my ancestors.
Humility to the process of re-membering.
My ancestors wish offerings, specific offerings,
honey and more rum.
I humble myself to the feet of my ancestors.

It was then that I casted the pattern that alerts me to completion, to clear acceptance of the offerings and to the closing of the ritual conversation. It was then that I understood that I needed to *shift* how I was with this unconventional call. That I needed to re-member myself in such a way that was not about conveying or proving or even explaining.

Vulnerability.

BlaC Altar

I am the steward.
I am responsive to who I re-remember to be,
to sur/rendering to the practice of re-membrance in action.
I am the visionary of realities I have yet to see,
art making practice in Black Love, in **BlaC** Care,
in abundance, in richness, in wholeness, in complexity, in vastness, in eternity.
Ifá, Òrúnmìlà, an òrìsà, divinity of wisdom of the Yorùbá peoples,
primordial force, ancient,
manifested as a human in the Blackest man.

BLaC was born when I was doula-ing my child in her dying process. The medical establishment gave her a short time to live after sustaining, what was diagnosed as an irreparable heart damage, after her very first chemo treatment. I was initiated into the decision of what my part would be in helping her die well and what code of ethics I would need to keep me accountable to my conviction in the flurry of life supporting machines and humans who work the intensive care units doing what they were trained to do. Their version of care was not sufficient for what my child needed and deserved. How could I care for my broken heart and hers right until the end without needing to bypass the shattering of our worlds and the grief that was present and lay in wait? What ancient codes did I have access to that would support me to be in collapse and despair while being present to the living aspect of the dying process? This period was one of the manifestations of **BLaC** as my own ethic for me and my beloved child, **Kaia De La Cruz Wil-**

liams. *This* is one of the ways that sur/rendering saved me and that Ifá saved me from death and saved me from childlessness (Abímbólá, 1975).

BLaC Life making in the face of constantly being chased by death and illness is what made the impossible possible. My relationship with seen and unseen forces has held me through all things impossible. **BlaC** Life must be politically engaged. It demands that I ask how and what care looks like for me and my relations in harmony with Mother Earth.

BlaC Altar

I am of the dreaming people...
The people whose vision comes from Dreams...
Cosmic breadcrumbs in my waking path...
I become responsible for the collective, for myself...
Sur/rendering... sensing... re-membering... affirming... activating... the mystery of dreamer medicine...
Consequences of "One Drop" ...
...

Blackness is technology...
Lessons from Father, Duncan Williams...

...
I am the craft and crafting of my becoming ...
I am the connection ... the Sur/Rendering... the relation...
I am the spiritual lineages' relationship to storytelling ...I am a storytelling keeper...
I am the living memory of those stories...
I am Senegalese Ballet...
I am Swahili... Orality ...
I am Duncan's daughter, Keshia
I am Ifá devotee, *Labalábà Awo Ìlúgùn*
I am art expressed in ceramics...
I am ancestral veneration...
I am the clashing, the smashing, the wailing and the smoothing of ecstatic grief and tranquil softening. I am healing...

REFERENCES

Abímbólá, W. (1975). *Sixteen great poems of Ifá*. UNESCO.
McGregor, A. O. (2018). *Patakis of the Orisha Tarot*. Llewellyn Publications.
Virtue, D. (2006). *Daily guidance from your Angels Oracle Cards*: Guidebook. Hay House Inc.
Williams, K. (2021). *The discovery initiative*. https://www.thediscoveryinitiative.org/
Williams, K. (2023). *Towards a Black lLove and cCare eEthic: Reimagining social work through the lens of Black tTechnologies.* Smith College Studies in Social Work. Manuscript Accepted Summer 2023.

... walking the forgotten path...

Miryam Espinosa-Dulanto

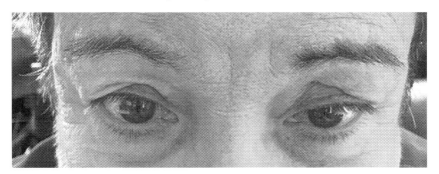

Today, I Turned 65

I halted for a moment.
I needed to remember when—in which one of all the crazy lives that I had to live,
in which of all those lives it happened
... paused to remember those lives with no other option but
    to go on
        ... move on,
in order to survive, in order to continue my life line
...
from born as a gift from the gods in a patriarchal state to learn how poverty shifts
    humans in piles of scum

... walking the path of displaced beings
... fearfully summoning to be scorned

Who Are You Without Colonialism? Pedagogies of Liberation, pages 131–133.
Copyright © 2023 by Information Age Publishing
www.infoagepub.com
All rights of reproduction in any form reserved.

… is that what colonialism makes one to be?

Not sure how to *name it…*
    colonialism, patriarchy, normality, love
… heard all those
    … whatever the name,
what I describe is the life of a young female in an ugly world
    … in a world policed and controlled by people different than her
    … where she needs to create a space even though she has the certainty it gonna fail
    … re-build it just to be dismembered, dream about it to simply be
            mercilessly awaken…
but each time,
    this young,
        not too young, now older woman
… gets ancestral energy and she tries again
…
each time,
she encounters few other displaced beings and   together/maybe   she/they   build something
    … maybe to
    … it doesn't matter, because is the try that counts
    … she/they don't know
    … she/they have no memory of other times
    … she/they have the yearn
    … the motivation
    … the desire of a different world
        where she/they will belong to

        where she/they will put roots

… and share their ancestral drive to be part of its re-creation
…

found
that i can't share
that nothing comes out from my mouth
that i sense people's forgotten experiences
followed by strand of tears
that pain and fear are shared
that i hear laughs and moans
pulling stomach flies
playing a dance
cuddling warm feelings
forgetting early agonies
soaking later passions

Without colonialism? Who am I?
I can share what is in my heart
… is the pain of being a tainted Mestiza,
a non-spoken Muchik[1],
born in the Global South,
heiress of a mixture of many races,
ethnicities,
worldviews—including the bloodthirsty of my own conditioning as a colonizer?
Yeah… you hear right
… that is the tainted inheritance of a Mestiza, contradictions, guilt and pride.

… the scream is silent
i do not recognize its sounds
the scream is full of past sounds
is full of unremembered words
it is echoing our impotent vocal cords
vocal cords able
to sound only the tyrants' languages
those foreign noises

REFERENCES

Anzaldua, G. (2012). *Borderlands / La frontera: The new mestiza* (4th ed.). Aunt Lute Books.

Arguedas, J. M. (1998). *Los Rios Profundos*. Bristol Classical Press.

Fanon, F. (1965). *The wretched of the earth*. Grove Press

Mohanty, C. T. (1984). Under Western eyes: Feminist scholarship and colonial discourses. *Boundary, 2*(12/13), 333–358. https://doi.org/10.2307/302821

Smith, L. T., Tuck, E., & Yang, K. W. (2018). *Indigenous and decolonizing studies in education: Mapping the long view.* Routledge

Spivak, G. C., & Young, R. (1991). Neocolonialism and the secret agent of knowledge. *Oxford Literary Review, 13*(1/2), 220–251. http://www.jstor.org/stable/43973717.

Vallejo, C. (1939/2010). Poemas humanos [Human Poems]. Linkgua, Kindle.

---

[1] The Muchik group settled along the northern coast and valleys of ancient Peru, in particular, in the Chicama and Trujillo Valleys, probably around 1 CE and 800 CE. This is my ancestral land, where I was raised, and my family settled.

A Micro-Essay on the "Micro-Essays on Poetics"

Octavio Quintanilla

On the peripheries of the page, not its right margin, or its center, is where I like to begin. It is where I make my first mark, reminding myself that with this act I want to do *something*, no matter how small, to destabilize what I've been taught to know about where the world begins, to say *No* to the god of prescription and order, and to say *Yes* to what I can't remember about my being.

Maybe doing this is an attempt to return to an origin that I feel is there, but that my knowing can't fully know. So much has been lost, after all. So many seeds trampled and burned, dried and scattered…

… there is still a seed in me that reaches towards the sunlight, that opens itself for rain. It no longer wants to be imprisoned by foreign notions of how to make beauty, how to write a poem, how to mark our emotional, spiritual, and intellectual lives on the page, on the canvas, on the skin.

Who Are You Without Colonialism? Pedagogies of Liberation, pages 135–136.
Copyright © 2023 by Information Age Publishing
www.infoagepub.com
All rights of reproduction in any form reserved.

To begin a poem in the peripheries of the page. To make a mark where no colonized mind would make a mark.

Look at the images throughout these pages. Can you tell where I began to write? Where will you begin to read? "Micro-Essays on Poetics #3, #8, #4, #2, #1, #7 or #9?"

I'm a Coast Salish Punjabi Settler and I am Not Okay

Sonia Das

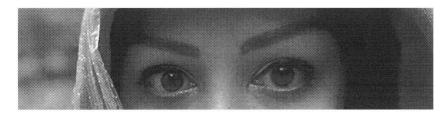

Unity is meaningless without the accompaniment of women. Education is fruitless without educated women and agitation is incomplete without the strength of women. Dr. B R Ambedkar

> Sing of my deeds
> Tell of my combats
> How I fought the treacherous demons
> Forgive my failings
> And bestow on me peace. Phoolan Devi

My deepest gratitude and Acknowledgements to my beloved co-conspirators that inspire me to walk a recovery path from colonialism. I couldn't have done this without your collective support of Direct Action and Unconditional Care:

Mom, Mejor Das, Arin Saxena, Mama Bear Pamela Lynne Chrisjohn and children, Ravi Saxena, Pooser, Bhajno Heer, Sarjit Heer, Palo Dass, Gurmej Kaur, New West, Harjeet Barring, Manroop Sandhu, Puth, Ekta Hattangady, Dr. Pavna

K Sodhi, Channdika Valli Thayver, Jyoti Solanki Davie, Anjali Walia Desure, JP Gratrix, Penpa Dolma, Emmy Chahal, Nirat Sohpaul, Jiddu Krishnamurti, Tupac Shakur, Roxane Gay, Toni Morrison, Angela Davis, Jyoti Singh and December 16, Thenmozhi Soundararajan, Dr. Ambedkar, Dr. Tania Ranwal, Dr. Meghna Bhat, The Battered Women's Support Society, The Downtown Eastside of Vancouver, The Haida Gwaii, Alok Menon, Dr. Gabor Mate, Lasagna Lady, Dr. Clelia O. Rodríguez, Dr. Josephine Gabi, My Boo, Miriam Hall, Balraj Dhillon, my beloved ancestors and to ALL survivors of cultural erasure and imperialism. I am forever in reciprocity of your radical love and selfless service towards Indigenous and Self Sovereignty.

May all be free from the oppressions of gender-based violence. May Indigenous Sovereignty be restored. My gratitude and solidarity is to the Land. May the Merits of Collective Wellbeing Accumulate to Free Minds, Bodies and Hearts from the terrifying shackles and effects of intergenerational genocide, racism, displacement of Indigenous peoples, incarceration, and all forms of violence.

The path is never finished.

"Even though you and I are in different canoes, in the River of Life, we are the same." What befalls me, befalls you."
—*Oren Lyons, Onondaga Nation Chief and member of the Indigenous Peoples of the Human Rights Commission of the United Nations*

Who am I without the colonizer's violence that has been digitized, globalized and embedded in my body? If I question it, I risk being stripped of all 'comforts' and 'FREEdoms'.

My family will scapegoat me and I will most likely not get accountability from them. They will label me as aggressive, hysterical, alcoholic, slut; they will silence me and ask why a child sits on a stranger's lap even though the child chooses not to. The supremacists will interrogate me, ask me where I live and who I love. They threatened my life with guns and bronze veneer it all. What are they hiding? What am I hiding?

Themselves. Violence. Religious propaganda. Missing Women. CHILDREN. Dead Children. Lies. Dishonored Treaties and Agreements. Money. Real Estate. Timber. War. Deception. Disrespect. The patriarchy winks behind the backs of our precious Indigenous Knowledge Keepers. They subject our beloved children to colonial poisons and pains, soothed in their adulthood by a glass of Crown Royal to chase down the pain like snake oil for the soul. I

drank the kkkool-aid and became deluded and complicit by misguided, performative allyship.

So if those are lies, what is Truth?

My community suffers from colonialism. The Indian caste system followed us over to the Unceded Indigenous territories of Turtle Island. I carry that trauma in my bones. This is why I inquired much deeper on the expression "what the fuck!" The question and political call of who I am without colonialism brings me to my family: My Great Grandparents migrated in 1904 from Punjab to the Salish Coast. My mom's father, Sarjit Heer Singh was born in the 1930s and was forced to assimilate on the unceded lands of the Cowichan people. He provided for his family driving logging trucks through Queen Charlotte Islands for British Columbia's chief forester and war administrator, Mr. Harvey Reginald McMillan.

I have observed throughout my entire life, a violent patriarchy emerging in many individuals I respected and loved, their behaviors morphing, contradicting and grasping for so-called "western privileges'" using colonizers' tools. I have often contemplated the treacherous labor men like my grandfather took on to try to earn extra and "get ahead". My grandfather comes to me in my dreams and affirms that my intuition on the world's state of madness, the ills and the harm colonization did and does to our family is True. The existential rage stemming from this realization comes in intergenerational waves—into my grandmother, into my mother, into me. The matriarchs feel the historical pain in their homes, on the land, where we learn to survive helping each other.

Deep down, in whatever was left, all I could do was hold onto faith and hope to find reconciliation along my stumbling path. I learned to get comfortable hiding love, putting on the mask of nihilism and following my individualistic mind that told me I must walk this path alone because no one was volunteering the truth I needed. I used my intelligence, charm and physical attractiveness to try to extract this truth—why were our children, women and lands treated so horribly? My half-assed attempt at liberating myself was telling the patriarch to Fuck off, and break silences, only to then mimic some of the very judgmental behavior I despised. With my colonialist beliefs and extraordinary sadness, I fearfully unleashed a wave that I had been running from my whole life to community on Instagram, a Zoom room full of educators, healers and kin in the hopes they would see me.

> I'm mocked for not being the Perfect Punjaban.
> Tell that to my Great Grandmothers and Ancestors.
> You hate me for my complex Punjabi Trauma Stress Disorder (c-PTSD).
> I hate you because you can't see why I am disordered.
> I have broken Punjabi but can feel the words of Urdu and Gurumukhi
> pierce through my spirit's vessel.
> I hate that I have been abused for religious and power advancements.
> I hate what the heteropatriarchy has done to themselves.
> God can't save the Queen.
> MLK didn't see that in his dream.
> Mom and the Matriarchs are the real Queens.
> They echo the repetitive genocidal screams.
> Raised by false Gurus who seek profits through prophets.
> Then garments are woven to deepen their pockets.
> Justin Trudeau and infiltrated markets.
> Pride for cash crops, they hear a gold rush.
> Kill and pillage, steal gold, then hushhhhhh.
> Ancestors forgotten and the sacrifices they made…

who picked up your children after unlawful slays.
Control, Conquer, Repeat, it made it to the streets.

I hate what colonialism has done to our Indigenous peoples and children.
I hate that I call it Queen Charlotte Island.
I hate that I call it British Columbia.
I hate that my Great Grandma was abandoned
I hate that my Grandmother was left behind in India with her two children while her husband was losing himself in British pubs and brothels.
I hate that my grandfather battered a Black man into a coma.
I hate that, as a result, my father had to quit school and kill mice to make money for his mother and siblings to pay for the small brick home with a fire stove in West Bromwich.
I hate that my father had no childhood.
I hate that my mother had no childhood.
I hate that my brother and I had no childhood after my father's family arrived.
I hate that I had no childhood because the pressures of liberating them all became a Boulder even Guru Nanak couldn't hold up.
I can't? won't deny my complicit involvement.
For I navigate those waters of pain each day.
I'm sorry Mother and Waters.
I'm sorry Mother and Waters.

Who Would I Be Without Colonialism?

I guarantee I would be without hate...

I would be wrapped in cotton cloth, with a dandelion, and cedar crown, foraging grabbing my grandmothers' hands, her chuckling for me to stop dancing around. I would wrap our heads with that Chiffon Chunni that flows like a kite in the wind, where I would remember my mother just like your old life back in the Pindh

I would be making pine tree potions and squeezing rose hips on my lips
I would soothe my wounds by reciting Om Namah Shiva while planting Bhang (cannabis)
for meditation in this world's relief
I would forage, heal with medicines and elixirs like Parvati did with her kid

It would be me being held in my complete grief and essential goodness
It's Grandma and the Elders teaching me how to make garments, cook and knit
It would mean being present for my baby
It would be me not worried how teachers treat our children behind bricked walls
It's support from the Elders when there is a spiritual crisis

Accountability and remorse for when a wrong has been committed
It would mean no more murdered and missing women and Two-Spirit people
It would mean me whirling for my beloved at the top of the Sarita River
It would mean meeting the love of my life and not have their white-collar parent discriminate
my status and economic condition

It would mean no more separation
It would mean for all to break all their silence
It would mean to protect the lands and treaties by any means necessary
It would mean we practice democracy
It would mean not having to compete and spend one hundred thousand on a wedding
It would mean giving up luxurious comforts
It means not being stopped by government officials at the "border" when I journey to see
my father
It would mean not getting abused, stalked, raped and coerced by community members
It would mean not exploiting others for drugs and money
It would mean being able to take my child to a karate class without a rub and tug next door
It would mean getting home safe when inebriated instead of having a penis inserted into the vagina when unconscious
It would mean career advancement without the celebrity chef asking me to suck his dick
It means me without anxiety and suicidal ideations
It means not conforming to late-stage imperialism
It means abolition in stigmas towards addicts and addiction
It means my father would have not been manipulated by men, caste,
family, and peers
It would mean a healed relationship with my mother
I would be Truth.

I am someone's child
I challenge the patriarchy
I transform poison into love
I fill my waters
I hold the belief of my own worth again...

Without colonialism, I would be happy to see children free to be themselves and the Matriarchs supported in their spiritual grief. For mothers to have their safety back, their families back, their lives back. Their children back. Their land back.

... : I am you : past : present : future : You are me : Lak'ech : ....

Clelia O. Rodríguez

Who echoed this oralized written call for action-based political living pedagogies manifested in my writing? Josephine Gabi, Ram Trikah, Anthonia Ikemeh, Fatema Rashed, Shauna Landsberg, Pamela Lynne Chrisjohn, Zahra Komelyan, Jihan Thomas, Miryam Espinosa-Dulanto, Odaymar Cuesta, Kathryn Sieber, Jackie Wing Tung Lee, Aquib S. Yacoob and Karin L. Lewis.

... : I am you : past : present : future : You are me : Lak'ech : Chintli : Faith : Pamela : Josephine : Glenda : Mary : Jihan : Anthony : Amanda : c.k. : Jackie : Shauna : Künsang: Danielle : Ram: Hope : Trung : Odaymar : Karthik : Zahra : Aquib : Anthazia : Kay : Miryam : Octavio : Chihera Shava Mhofu : doro remasese : Mwari Musiki: pfuko : Ivhu kuvhu : Ubuntu : Pamela : O:nenhste : Yethi'nihstenha Onhwentsyakekha : Aksotha : Niin : Indaanikoobijigan : Nimishoomis : Nookomis

: Noos : Ninga : Niin : Ningozis : Nindaanis : Noozhishenh : Indaanikoobijigan : Indinawemaaganidog : Mino-bimaadiziwin : Bimaadizi : Gichi-dibaakonigewinan : Opwaagan : Asemaa : Bashkodejiibik : Wiingashk : Giizhik : Gichi-aya'aa : Mindi-mooyenh : Yethi'nihstenha Onhwentsyakekha : O:nenhste : Aksotha : Debwewin : Dabasendizowin : Manaaji'idiwin : Zaagi'idiwin : Zoongide'ewin : Gwayakwaadiziwin : Nibwaakaawin : Annji-Bimaadizing : Aanikegamaa : Aanikobidoon : Akiwenzii : Cintli : tlālli : the anatomy of a being in stillness : sounds to be tasted : tastes to be felt : writing to be watered : ecology that boils love : echoes waiting to turn to echoing : translations to be destroyed : interpretations to be created : a child in transition to be remembered : a sharpened ear : shield of silence : constellations among constellations : cipotada jugando arranca cebollas : the nature of writing fertilized in imagination : the possibility of gymtastics in Algebra : the continuity of bees : nests on nests : branching on the shoulders of Fire : an orbit with no beginning or end : the living walking spirit of ancestral mathematics : spiral : spiralling : secrets waiting to be whispered when I transition : the given Truth of the reflection of a seed : a cascade of tears turned pearls : a geometrical chaos within a geometrical order : a horse named Cirilo : the solar system's dusty embryo : light in stillness : the secret way of corn : the location of reciprocity in the Universe : a hope written in Latin : velut arbor aevo : an aspiring harmonizer : a visionary of the past : a Lioness : a recording of another galaxy : 7 : a memorable historical smile : pollinator : cross-pollinator : a traveling radar without a compas : 30,000 year-old honey : seaweed : shadow among shadows :

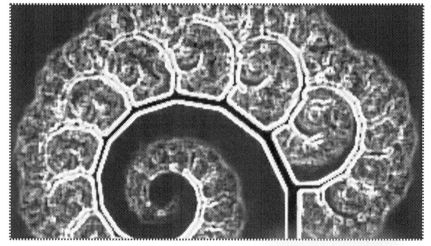

... : I am you : past : present : future : You are me : Lak'ech : .... • 145

Clelia, the snake : Clelia, a once-upon-a-time Etruscan woman whose Liberation came from water : rivers in the sky : humility in front of a butterfly : a point of the unknown : a known point : the fractal geometrical of my reflection I leave in this book : the balsam that blesses each voice I welcome here : the intersection of bells: a question mark on a tomb : a living underground oasis of possibilities : you : ...

Pedagogies of Liberation are Tongue Sovereignty. That is where the memory of land rests empowered in my belly button. The seed of this living book comes from a volcanic cauldron located in my chest and it is burning. It gives me life and nears me to death. The seed was awaken abruptly by greed. It was nasty, brutal, and a vivid reminder that colonialism, despite ongoing efforts to 'decolonize' this and 'decolonize' that, stands on the shoulders of emptie boxes. The Tongue I carry was sharpened by my Grandfather's machete. Filudo. Filudo. Filudo. For every person that approaches this work, that is sacred, with the pretense to 'take-away', know this: You will not experience eviction because you will never flourish in these lands. Weeding out is active. Healing is political work, is political work, is political work. Carry the 3x as a formula in your backpack. Some of you are really operating like marketing officers for pharmaceutical companies taking away medicine just to contaminated with white feminism et al.

Pedagogies of Liberation are life: Lungs. I cannot breathe in front of those whose colonized hearts interrupt my love for Death. The exclamations marks forced without any anesthesia from my light is spiritual violence. Those whose notions of gratitude falls flat following an immediate "thank you for the takeaways." This ain't no buffet nor a la carte menu. Nor it is a stop-over to fill-up the empty machine you're carrying in the name of 'progress.' I cannot be liberated until political listening is figured out when you stop the capitalist cycle of rampage consumption of space, place, presence, air and energy. Even Zoom is depleted at this point. You can have 'decolonization' because it is dead. The killing of spirit is real, alive and there isn't enough standing trees to give shade to shade. The pair of trees I carry are heavy. They are yours too. My death is your responsibility. My life is your responsibility.

Pedagogies of Liberation as in James Baldwin is in land: "How much time do you want for your progress?"—the possibility of Liberation is not a path made of cotton candy. Its characteristics are specifics: Loud, rough, joyous, spider-like webbing, dense, prefaced by lighting, an umbral that turns when healing knocks the door, calibrated hair with the power of braiding, universal-scales of thirst for Dignity, and an army of seekers of Liberation. To carry forward this political pedagogical work has meant falls, bruises, tears, sweat, heart palpitations… and each feeling I am now choosing to forget to deliver this collective work under the inquisitorial question of 'who are you without colonialism', was charged by Catabumbo lighting. Baldwin's Knowledge is like the spirit of Thunder made visible in the skies from my Ancestors. Is in the skies where Truth is seen. To grasp, even if it's just for fragments of seconds, the intensity of this land-based pedagogy simply locate my writing at 8°30′N 71°0′W and 9°45′N 73°0′W on Google Maps. Know the perimeter of boundaries because we are striking to the rhythm of the Land. She is angry. So am I.

Pedagogies of Liberation as in Audre Lorde: Are you seriously still speaking of sitting at the table and representation? We are PRESENCE. Blowing one's existence instantly to occupy a space that is an illusion is our destination to disaster. Liberation is in the LAND. The tools are waiting to be picked up from where they were left out. Turn around. Abandon the house. That path was always the wrong way. You are needed to protect the shade of your shadow. I speak to you, conscious listener of your own blood flow, the one that shakes you preventing the silencing of the an Ancestral whisper. And when I say Ancestors, I include all of them. The good and bad. The ones that caged the uterus before mine. The ones that embodied darkness to THAT point of no return. That is what's up in Elmina Castle. The ones that still believe that progress comes from the shenanigans of branding. Poor cows. I remember the smell of burning skin spreading like wildfires. If you don't mark them with this *fierro*, the cattle branding unique iron, no one will credit them as private property. That is when I learned what is behind today's obnoxious politics of IDentity, which I translate within the confiments of English to those in 'higher' learning spaces. The marks that captivate the superlative form in 'higher' visualizes that lesson that I now pass on to you.

One blackboard, two chairs, and fosforecent lighting. This photograph was taken with the radical hope of Life beyond deadlines at 252 Bloor Street West in the building of the Ontario Institute for Studies in Education and it reminds me that white violence is the sugar that keeps Caste and Class as the NEWest elephant in the room. It is my Knowledge transcribed in the English Langauge.

The knots and bolts that marked the beginning of the journey of my ancestral seed that now materializes in an ecology of pedagogies based on teachings of the land, was echoed by Dr. Josephine Gabi: Let us address the elephant in the room! #WeAreNotOkay. To listen politically means to follow the sensorial path of the umbilical cord that connects us to the womb, to the land. To teach and learn beyond the binary is a conscious, CONSCIOUS, conscious awareness where the Truth of burned skin is part of a daily prayer. Know language. Know math. Polical economists trying to make sense of poverty are reproducing stagnation with language. How much more RE-search is required to return the seeds and food security you take and take to make sense of statistics. How many more times do we need to put up with the psychological impact of activities marketed as 'discovery,' 'explore,' and 'expertise'? Your math is limited and we, stewards of

148 • CLELIA O. RODRÍGUEZ

ancestral math, have the answers to the equation of the square root of justice. You are simply choosing not to listen.

Those who are after Pedagogies of Liberation as dreamt, as manifested, as lived and as experienced and as Defensors of Seeds of Indigenous Knowledge, learn from Zero the multi-generational responsonsabilities what this work is and is not about. Zero embodied in the snail. Zero embodied in a seed. We are not here to serve masturbation-based, extractivist-educational colonialist protocols and take-away approaches whose agendas pollute the body and mind. No. Subjectivity no more. Respect. Without it, #EveryChildMatters is just anoter commercialized date that white violence protectors are rushing to to grab to get into educational programs, to apply for prestigious grants and to get jobs. DISrespect. I heart-mind the cascading ancestral anger echoing the spirit of Thunder:

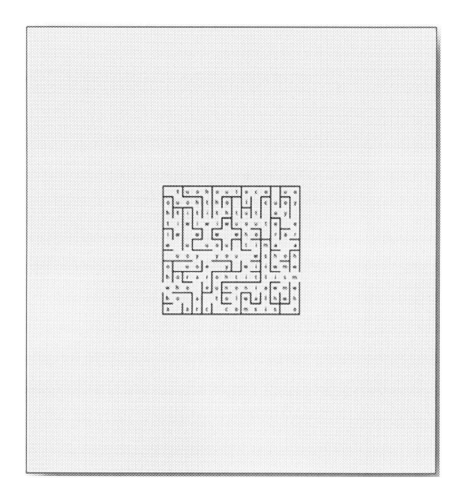

"White lady,
Did I just hear you correctly?
No! STOP! Do not speak to us that way!
We don't want you here.
You know what, white people? You've had your voice here for 524 years.
Five hundred and twenty-four years you've been visible, white lady ... Look how fast your white man comes and stands up for you. Where is everybody else to come and stand up for us?
Look how many people came to bat for you, white lady. And you're a guest here. Without us, you'd be homeless. This is over." Elder Jocelyn Wabano-Iahtail

Tetonalli—Nuevo comienzo ... new beginning ...

Bios/Statements From Contributors

Amanda Buffalo

I have centred my community role on supporting the sustainability of Indigenous communities in a variety of fields, though my focus has been on working with communities to address violence and the impacts of hetero-patriarchy and settler-colonialism on communities, community development, education, health, and governance/leadership. I dedicate my time to supporting both community-based and global approaches to Indigenous people's social, political, legal, and economic equity and equality, and am honoured to have had a community role in working directly with families of Missing and Murdered Indigenous Women and Girls and survivors of violence (locally and nationally). Though I am working to develop my skills as a connoisseur of tea, bannock, and dry meat, I still have much to learn and my many teachers continue to support me in learning about my role(s) and responsibilities in passing on culture, tradition, and language.

Email: amanda.buffalo@live.ca

Mary R. Chakasim

B.A., LL.B., LL.L. Mary is Omushkego from Moosonee, Ontario and a member of Attawapiskat First Nation. Mary was raised by her grandparents, Sympharien & Madeline (nee Sutherland) Chakasim, both survivors of St. Anne's residential school; her mother Maria, and aunts, Annabella and Noella. She is mother to Neegahnii, Danasco, & Mattinaway. Mary is a lawyer, mediator, policy developer, equity, diversity & inclusion education creator and provider, and human rights and human trafficking prevention education provider. Due to faith in 'alternate' forms of education and traditional forms of instruction based on connection to family and community, she 'unschooled' her daughters since birth. She hopes to contribute to the growing inventory of written text confirming the validity of traditional knowledge and methodologies, through the merger of current technology and traditional activity and philosophy for curriculum creation, beginning with the task of documenting traditional law from story.

Email: mchakasim71@gmail.com

Pamela Lynne Chrisjohn

Pamela Lynne Chrisjohn is an eclectic Onyota'a:ka/Oneida (People of the Standing Stone) visual artist, a Haudenosaunee (Person of the Longhouse) from the Oneida Settlement, which is a sovereign territory within Canadian borders. The homelands are the finger lakes region of what is now Upper New York State, the Onyota'a:ka established themselves along the Thames River in Upper Canada in 1840. Being a matriarch to five life givers is a fierce responsibility which she takes very seriously. The creative concepts Pamela gathers and weaves in her paintings, photography, writing, and beadwork are becoming a fruitful basket overflowing with collective cultural knowledge. Just as so many have done before her, the goal is to maintain and share the teachings of elders and ancestors for future Onkwehonwe (the original people) generations. Her gift of a creative imagination can be most recently seen as a 7-foot banners spanning the Mercier Bridge in Montreal, Quebec.

Email: pamela.lynne.chrisjohn@gmail.com

Odaymar Cuesta

Odaymar is an active afrocuban multidisciplinary transfeminist inmigrant, artivist, musician, poet, performer, organizer, educator, author, visual artist, born in Havana Cuba in the seventies and now Oakland California resident. Odaymar studied Fine Arts the Higher Pedagogical Institute in Habana Cuba and in 1999 cofounded Krudas (Krudxs) Cubensi a queer feminist Afro Cuban Hip-Hop band that stand up for Black and Brown People, Women, Trans people, Gender nonconforming People, Queer people, Immigrants and the struggles and claims of all intersectional beings. krudascubensi.com

The band brings knowledge, powerful and crispy flow, authentic afroCaribbean sounds like dancehall, reggae, trap and super dope afrolatin hip hop beats to uplifting confidence, heavy pride, sexiness, rebellion, truth and decolonial lyrics. They chose music as their weapon to celebrate life and fight against oppression because through art change happens. Music is like water, everybody needs it. From 1999 until today Krudas have been working uninterruptedly offering art and knowledge with over two hundred original songs, more than five hundred performances and more than two hundred workshops and talks across universities and colleges in the United States. They have been a prestigious Astraea Foundation Global Arts Fund grantee (2017), awarded the Best Hip Hop Video at the Lucas Video Awards in Havana, Cuba (2016), and Artists-in-Residence at allgo.org one of Texas's oldest statewide queer people of color organizations (2015—2021) and the Queer Hip Hop Cypher (Park Avenue Armory) are Bessie Award nominated Outstanding Performer in 2022.. Krudas have performed in the First Avenue Theatre in Minneapolis, MN, SOB's NY, Brava Theatre SF, Kennedy Center for Performing Arts in Washington D.C, Mission Cultural Center SF, The Fillmore Miami Beach Fl, SXSW Film and Music Festival Austin TX, Lincoln Center NYC. The Krudxs documentary *Somos Krudas* produced by Arts in Context with PBS won the Best Topic Lone Star Emmy Award in Austin, TX in 2015. In the 2021–2022 school year they were selected as artist fellows of the Abolition Democracy Fellow Program in the Black Studies Collaboratory at the University of California Berkeley.

Email: cuestaodaymara@gmail.com

Hope Andromeda Kitts

Soy juera. Soy Burqueña. Cuando yo era niña me llamaban "pinche juera." I was a pinche juera. Internalizing false superiority I enacted the colonizer's gaze, judgement, affect. I remember at six years old, as I was too obviously admiring a wedding party, a flower girl approached me to say, "You wanna fight?" It's taken me a lifetime to understand that interaction, to understand how others' interpret my body. This journey has led me to question my embodiment in the context of historical unfolding. In the tradition of Vipassana, as taught to me by my teacher S.N. Goenka, I recognize that in reality there is no "Dr. Hope Andromeda Kitts," rather "I" am an illusion, a mirage, a collection of vibrations here for a splitsecond, a visitor here to break curses before melting back into oneness. While I am here, in this body, I research, write and teach about white identity for the sake of its dismantling, for the sake of turning the beast on its master. This personal journey, beginning in the junk heap my grandmother rescued me from, has led to my work as Assistant Professor in the department of Education at the University of Minnesota-Duluth. "I" teach undergraduate liberal education courses on the social construction of white identity, human diversity and antiracist and inclusive schooling for future elementary school teachers. Today, I am likely still a pinche juera, though hopefully a more conscious, less defensive one. And, 34 years later, to that descriptor I add: Mother to Walt and Bill, partner to James, and co-conspiring race traitor.

   Email: hkitts@d.umn.edu
   https://andromedakitts.wordpress.com/

Danielle Denichaud

There is no singular response to this query, for while I, Danielle Denichaud, am the composer of this current form of expression, I am not the creator of this offering. It has been growing my entire embodied life, and so carries the imprint of every relationship and walk on grass, each tree climbed and lake swum, each cloud gazed and star sky dreamed to. My ancestors are present too. I may not know their names yet their songs live through me; calling me to dance beneath the moon and awaken early to pray with the sun's rise on our Earth horizon. They beckon me forward through the dark of these times, to sing into the storm and dance these feet into concrete until the path is cleared for Life to thrive again. I also honour the more-than-human me that I am; the bacteria, parasite, fungi and viruses that inhabit the same fleshy, liquid, tendonous, bony terrain of this body home. What is their role in the creation of these thoughts, expressions, movements and sounds? And what of the soil, sun, water, air and spaciousness enlivening me since the beginning of me? They too are credited with the inspirations shared here within. Aho.

   Email: d.denichaud@mail.utoronto.ca
   IG: @lightonhealth

Miryam Espinosa-Dulanto

She is a faculty member, serving in a regional university, at the USA/Mexico border. There, in a largely minoritized area, Miryam connects her community service with her teaching and research. Academically, Miryam draws on decolonial indigenous feminist research methodologies, yet it is the community connection that collaboratively produces and shares the poetry, testimonios, ethnography and art-based qualitative methodologies.

   Email: miryam.espinosadulanto@utrgv.edu

Josephine Gabi

She (Her/Hers) is a Reader in Education at Manchester Metropolitan University. Grounded in Black feminist thought, and antiracist praxis, she is dedicated to challenging disembodied pedagogy in the early year's education and care and undoing forms of coloniality in curricula and relational encounters. Josephine embraces solidarity as a tool of resistance to the matrix of domination as a critical orientation towards liberated futures. Her work advances co-creation as a liberatory pedagogy that facilitates relational agency. Josephine is a Senior Advisor of the UK Advising and Tutoring (UKAT) and a Senior Fellow of the Higher Education Academy (AdvanceHE).

Email: j.gabi@mmu.ac.uk

Anthazia Kadir

Rooted in the entanglements of Caribbean cultures and discourses, Anthazia is an educator, author, poet, narrative researcher and storyteller who intentionally brings her heart and wisdom into her practice. She holds an M.Ed. in Curriculum and Instruction and is trained in Narrative Therapy and Meaning Making. Anthazia values research and teaching as relational practices. She works through the intersections of decolonization, transformative curriculum practices, teacher education reform, radical contemplative pedagogies, grief, healing and narrative mindfulness. Anthazia has spent over 20 years in the classroom and has collaborated with several community organizations and universities. Some of her collaborations include one of Canada's oldest magazines, The Fiddlehead, through the University of New Brunswick, where she founded in 2018 Arrivals and Departures, intended for immigrants to share their stories about treasured objects, loss, longing and making anew. She has also done narrative work with museums and seniors living through their third acts. Through the St. Thomas University, Fredericton, NB, where Anthazia is a member of the Centre for Interdisciplinary Research—Narrative, she is involved in a book project focusing on cherished objects and storytelling. Amidst Anthazia's travels and the invaluable experiences these journeys have gifted her, her renewal often comes from her collaborations with others in her field. Currently, Anthazia offers healing re-storying conversations as a guest lecturer at universities, conference presentations, and embodied narrative workshops for seniors, educators and students.

Email: anzia.jorna@gmail.com

Zahra Komeylian

Shis an Iranian artist and educator based in Tkaronto/Toronto. Komeylian's artistic practice is grounded in self-reflexive processes and slow methodologies. Working in performance art, sculpture-installation, text, and drawing, her works inform one another in circularity. Komeylian's research contends with personal myth and autotheory, embodied knowledge, collective symbology (archetype). Her pedagogical practice draws heavily on creative self-inquiry. Komeylian holds an MA in Psychology (2017) from Columbia University and Master of Teaching (2023) from OISE, University of Toronto. She has exhibited her work globally.

Tenzin Künsang (she, her)

Name: Tenzin means upholder of the Buddha's teachings. Künsang refers to the Bodhisattva Samantabhadra. Tenzin Künsang is a Tibetan name.
　Aspiration: Teach compassion and guide ways for cultivating it.
　Conventional bio: Former instructor of English as a foreign language.
　Relative bio: Tibetan Buddhist, transcultural Asian American, spiritual friend, seeker, dreamer, wanderer, creator and destroyer of my delusions, mental health advocate, BTS ARMY.
　Spiritual bio: Tibetan Buddhist philosophy is my foundation and core principle on the path of liberation. In my past lives, I studied and practiced the wisdom and compassion of my Indian and Tibetan spiritual ancestors. Before that, I may have lived as a turtle, tiger, butterfly, soldier, and more. I may have been your brother, sister, mother, father, or grandparent. I may have saved your life. I may have been your oppressor. In this present life, I was reborn in Asia again—28 years after colonial rule ended in my birth country; 20 years after a war; and during another year of an authoritarian, military government. The knowledge holders of my spiritual tradition and lineage are from Tibet. The land of Tibet is colonized. Tibetans in Tibet are living with colonial oppression, systemic cultural genocide, and human rights violations. These include psychological warfare, media warfare, forced DNA collection, torture, separation of one million Tibetan children from their families and being forced into colonial boarding schools, and discrediting the Dalai Lama to the world. The colonizer has been replacing the Tibetan culture, knowledge, history, and spiritual lineages with their stories. My parents, spiritual ancestors and teachers of India and Tibet, and the Tibetan people have been life-saving and life-giving to liberate my mind. They have been influencing my capacity to help people and any compassion that I may have grown. My intentions and actions in this lifetime plant the seeds for the next rebirth to reunite with my spiritual ancestors and teachers again and again to continue the work for the benefit of sentient beings and liberation of their minds.
　May the wisdom and understanding that I lack and do not know arise and grow.

Shauna Landsberg

Shauna Landsberg (she/her) <Shoshanna bat Rueben Pesach> daughter, sister, aunt, knitter, community colearner/unlearner, and 4th generation Ashkenazi Jewish settler in Tkaronto, Canada. After receiving a B.A. from Western Kentucky University, Shauna began her public-school teaching career with the Nashville Teaching Fellows—The New Teacher Project (TNTP). She spent four years learning alongside English Language Learners and early elementary students and was a founding teacher at Purpose Preparatory Academy, currently ranked as the best Nashville elementary school for Black and economically oppressed students. In 2015, ancestral whispers motivated Shauna to move to Tkaronto and live near her last remaining grandparent by blood, June Landsberg Weinberg. Shauna is now an Ontario Certified Teacher (OCT), intending to graduate from the Master of Teaching program at OISE, University of Toronto, in November 2023. Through an elective course at OISE, Shauna joined SEEDS for Change, a global learning collective founded by Dr. Clelia Rodriguez. She answers the call, "Who are you without colonialism?" through a process of ancestral healing as the necessary ritual toward a liberatory future and sustaining reciprocity with the land and its traditional stewards, the Haudenosaunee, Anishinabek, Huron Wendat and Mississaugas of the Credit. By tracing her Truth, colonizer, assimilator, member of a diasporic minority, Jewish cis woman, she aims to weave pedagogies of liberation with learners of all ages that honor the work of Black, Brown, indigenous, queer, female, trans, plant, animal, and celestial ancestors of past, present, and future. She is now working to become a Primary/Junior teacher in the Toronto District School Board, where she hopes her journey resonates with and nourish students in their educational journey.

Email: shauna.landsberg@gmail.com

李詠彤 *(Lee Wing Tung)*

My name is Jackie Lee and my Chinese name is 李詠彤 (Lee Wing Tung). Pronouns are she, her, and hers. If you do not speak my native tongue, Cantonese, you can just call me Jackie. I was born and raised in a colonized and highly politicalized land. My family and I moved to this colonized land (also known as Canada) and resided in what we now call Toronto when I was 11 years old. I speak three languages, one of which will go extinct in the next few decades. I work as a public educator and my battlefield is in a public library. If I am not at work, you might find me drawing, cooking, eating, breathing, or, advocating. Life is political, and politics are life.

Email: jackieclee@live.com

Glenda Mejía

Glenda is a scholar and an educator born in El Salvador. She teaches in the field of migration/mobility/displacement, and Spanish language/culture studies at RMIT's School of Global, Urban and Social Studies, recognising the university as a colonised spaced and unceded sovereignty of the Traditional Custodians of the Kulin Nations on which she lives, works and breathes. I extend that respect to Elders past, present and emerging as well as Aboriginal and Torres Strait Islander peoples throughout Australia. As an educator and a scholar, Glenda is committed to un/re/learning and teaching by engaging and embodying a praxis of decolonising approaches, senti-pensante and liberation pedagogies. Her ethics, teaching, and work are inspired by Gloria Anzaldúa, bell hooks, Clelia O. Rodríguez, and Paulo Freire. Some of her work and publications cover topics on inclusive language in the Spanish language classroom, experiences and memories of Latin American (Im)migrants and displaced people in Australia. She is currently working on an arts-based community participatory practice titled 'Storytelling displacement: Salvadoreans' memories in Australia.' She is a member of AILASA (Association of Iberian and Latin American Studies of Australasia) and LCNAU (Languages and Cultures Network for Australian Universities).

Email: glenda.mejia@rmit.edu.au

Web page https://www.rmit.edu.au/contact/staff-contacts/academic-staff/m/mejia-dr-glenda

Faith Mkwesha

She is a Zimbabwean of the Chihera shava mhofu totem currently living in Finland. She is a mother and a grandmother who is passionate about decolonising education and decolonising knowledges. Her motherhood inspires her work as she strives for equality and human rights for everyone. She is the founder of SahWira Africa International NGO, a Black feminist organisation, that advocates for the protection of Black children and access to equal quality education. As a social justice warrior, she works launching campaigns to influence policy change to end racism and discrimination: ProtectBlackGirlsToo #PtotectBlackChildren #Negro/Negre/Neekeritisracist,Hitlerswastika #NoRacismInUniversity #WeAreNotSkinColour

She is a researcher and lecturer at Helsinki University, the Swedish School of Social Sciences, The Centre of Ethnic Relations and Nationalism (CEREN) in Finland. She completed her multidisciplinary PhD at Stellenbosch University in South Africa on representations of gender and nation in Zimbabwe and African literature and culture from a postcolonial perspective. She is interested in disobedient-based knowledges, teaches Contemporary research methodologies, decolonising knowledges, minority studies, black/African feminism, African literature. Also, one of the editors of the book *Rasismi, valta ja vastarinta: rodullistaminen, valkoisuus ja koloniaalisuus Suomessa*, English: *Racism, power and resistance: Racialization, whiteness and colonialism in Finland.*

Emai: faithmk20@gmail.com

Trung M. Nguyễn

(she/he/they) is a Ph.D. student in Women, Gender, and Sexuality at Oregon State University, with minors in Ethnic Studies and Queer Studies. They earned their MAs in Performance Studies and TESOL at New York University and The New School, respectively. Entrenched in interdisciplinarity, their research and arts practices focus on feminist queer and trans studies in Southeast Asia. Their dissertation will explore the indigeneity of Vietnamese marginalized gender subjects in Vietnam through various critical lenses of film studies, postcolonial critiques, and queer theories.

Email: trung.nguyen@oregonstate.edu

Octavio Quintanilla

Octavio Quintanilla is the author of the poetry collection, *If I Go Missing* (Slough Press, 2014) and served as the 2018–2020 Poet Laureate of San Antonio, TX. His poetry, fiction, translations, and photography have appeared, or are forthcoming, in journals such as *Salamander, RHINO, Alaska Quarterly Review, Pilgrimage, Green Mountains Review, Southwestern American Literature, The Texas Observer, Existere: A Journal of Art & Literature,* and elsewhere. His Frontextos (visual poems) have been published in *Poetry Northwest, Borderlands: Texas Poetry Review, Midway Journal, Gold Wake Live, Newfound, Chachalaca Review, Chair Poetry Evenings, Red Wedge, The Museum of Americana, About Place Journal, The American Journal of Poetry, The Windward Review, Tapestry, Twisted Vine Literary Arts Journal,* & *The Langdon Review of the Arts in Texas.*

Octavio's visual work has been exhibited at the Southwest School of Art, Presa House Gallery, Brownsville Museum of Fine Art, Equinox Gallery, The University of Texas—Rio Grande Valley (Brownsville Campus), the Weslaco Museum, Aanna Reyes Gallery, Our Lady of the Lake University, AllState Almaguer art space in Mission, TX, El Centro Cultural Hispano de San Marcos, The Walker's Gallery in San Marcos, TX, and in the Emma S. Barrientos Mexican American Cultural Center / Black Box Theater in Austin, TX. A new series of work was exhibited in the Brownsville Museum of Fine Art in July, 2021. He holds a Ph.D. from the University of North Texas and is the regional editor for *Texas Books in Review* and poetry editor for *The Journal of Latina Critical Feminism* & for *Voices de la Luna: A Quarterly Literature & Arts Magazine.* Octavio teaches Literature and Creative Writing in the M.A./M.F.A. program at Our Lady of the Lake University in San Antonio, Texas.

Website: octavioquintanilla.com
Instagram @writeroctavioquintanilla
Twitter @OctQuintanilla

Clelia O. Rodríguez

IG: clelia.o.rodriguez / seedsforchange.ca
https://www.seedsforchange.ca/

c.k. samuels

jambican studio gardens (owner). BA Administrative and Commercial Studies in Social Organization and Human Relations, 1990. I am Blessed with land on which I can grow vegetables and flowers, commune with trees young and old, observe and attract wildlife of all kinds. I can quiet the madness attacking my soul and embrace the peace of being 'closer to wild'. Embracing the wild is comfort for the soul. The wild is the soul's surroundings. I have written and performed poetry with and without music since the early 1990s. As a multi-instrumentalist, I have played and toured with Ottawa-based bands. Music and poetry manifest similarly, sparked by anger, beauty, intense emotions, and observations. Much to be collected, much to resolve. Complexities to be embraced, simplicities to be found. All of this applies also to land stewardship inside of commercial environments. Observation with intent, meaning I know what I want to happen, my desired results, and I am watching to see how the land environment reacts to my (and others) desires as manifested through our actions. Call and response.

Email: jambicansg@gmail.com

Sonia Das Saxena

Sonia is a mother, domestic/sexual violence warrior, poet, entrepreneur and a radical love steward amongst many other identities. She is a fourth generation Punjabi settler born and raised on the unceded lands of the Coast Salish Peoples. One day at a time she is committed in honoring the ancestors of the lands she resides on and in reverence is actively alchemizing colonial mind poisons to re imagine a liberated world for our children. One where ALL those historically met with violence are rehabilitated and restored back to their sacred ways, families and communities.

Email: soniasaxena1118@gmail.com

Jihan A. Thomas

Jihan is a visual artist, Artivist, Mother, and community/museum arts educator based in Philadelphia, Pennsylvania, U.S.A. She uses her art and creativity to serve her city and community through art making experiences. To Jihan, art can be a conduit for empowerment, self-actualization and self reflection. As an art educator, Jihan is fully invested in dispelling Anti Blackness within art education and visual culture as it effects Black people and the Global majority. Jihan believes in the power of Black imagination, rematriation, joy and rebellion ideologies. Jihan has been the Museum Education Division Director for the Pennsylvania Art Education Association and has also created art programing and curriculum for the

African American Museum in Philadelphia, The School District of Philadelphia, The Philadelphia Museum of Art, and The Barnes Foundation.
Email: tns86@yahoo.com
Website: http://www.originalseedexpressions.com/

Ram Trikha

Born and raised in Markham, Ontario. He is an educator, music producer, creator, and lifelong learner. He seeks to constantly (un)learn, express himself in various art forms, and bring his passions for hip hop and social justice into the classroom.
IG: @trix.the.kid
Email @ramtrikha98@gmail.com

Karthik Vigneswaran (he/him)

First Generation Tamil settler in Tkaronto (Toronto, Ontario, Canada). He completed B.Sc in Biomedical Sciences at Toronto Metropolitan University. Started teaching from a young age: Tamil tutor, STEM subject tutor, Swim Instructor and First Aid Instructor. Early on, he became fascinated with the different ways science education is conducted. Karthik began working with at-risk youth in STEM subjects which allowed him to explore the pedagogical tools of mindfulness, nature therapy, well-being and cultural integration in education. Karthik continued his pedagogical venture at OISE earning a Master of Education in Curriculum and Pedagogy, where his academic focus was the intercultural integration of STEM curriculums. Currently, Karthik works as a STEM teacher in Tkaronto with the professional intention of working with different cultural groups, and to make STEM curriculums more relevant and holistic to the individual learner.
Email: k.vigneswaran@mail.utoronto.ca

Kay (Keshia) Williams

Labalábá is the daughter of Duncan and Donna; the fierce mother and steward of Kaia; a cherished descendant of my ancestors, indigenous African peoples, and a humble devotee of Ifá as it is practiced by the traditional Yorùbá of Yorùbáland. I have made this written offering from the ancestral and traditional lands of the Mississauga of Scugog Island. I am a madquestionasking steward of Black Love and Care who throws ceramic pots as a form of altar building. I am committed to the project of learning how to mind the business of my life. I am learning how to listen deeply to the teachings life continues to offer me. Email: kay.williams@thediscoveryinitiative.org

Aquib S. Yacoob.

Guided by Paulo Freire's "Pedagogy of the Oppressed" and the dope aunties in his life, Aquib S. Yacoob is a community organizer, strategist, and "fixer" utilizing the arts and culture as vehicles to (re)claim power in communities oppressed by difference. He is currently a scholar at Rice University, where his work includes radical experimentation for funding community-driven social change. Aquib Yacoob grew up in a small sugar plantation community in Guyana. He went to bed scared most of his childhood—jumping awake each time a mango fell on his rusty zinc roof. When his family immigrated to NYC in 2001, mangos on the roof were replaced by bullets in the night sky. From age 14, in a passionate search for safety and security, he began developing human rights campaigns and training organizers with Amnesty International. A decade later, he joined Women's March, mobilizing millions and planting seeds for transformation across his communities. When his childhood neighborhood saw 30+ shootings in 2019, he joined forces with a local organizer and, together, scaled her community-led gun violence solution to a $5B commitment from the White House. However, after each win, he notes returning to the same realization: the non-profit model alone cannot create the structural, root-level changes his communities need. True change comes from the wisdom of everyday people, held up by the dirt under our feet and alive in the air that fills our lungs.

   Email: aquib@brownmanrunning.com